Son of Yahweh

The Gospels as Novels

Son of Yahweh

The Gospels as Novels

Clarke W. Owens

CHRISTIAN
ALTERNATIVE

Winchester, UK
Washington, USA

First published by Christian Alternative Books, 2013
Christian Alternative Books is an imprint of John Hunt Publishing Ltd.,
Laurel House, Station Approach,
Alresford, Hants, SO24 9JH, UK
office1@jhpbooks.net
www.johnhuntpublishing.com
www.christian-alternative.com

For distributor details and how to order please visit the 'Ordering' section on our website.

Text copyright: Clarke W. Owens 2013

ISBN: 978 1 78279 067 9

A CIP catalogue record for this book is available from the British Library.

Design: Stuart Davies

Printed and bound by CPI Group (UK) Ltd, Croydon, CR0 4YY

We operate a distinctive and ethical publishing philosophy in all areas of our business, from our global network of authors to production and worldwide distribution.

CONTENTS

Acknowledgements

The author gratefully acknowledges the permission of Polebridge Press to quote liberally from Robert J. Miller, ed., *The Complete Gospels: Annotated Scholars Version*, 1992, 1994. Except where noted, gospel quotations are from this source, referred to herein as the ASV.

Non-gospel Biblical quotations are from *The New English Bible with the Apocrypha*, NY: Cambridge UP 1972, unless noted otherwise.

Thanks to Jeri Studebaker for advice and encouragement.

This book is for D, who can identify.

Introduction

When we read fiction, we assess plausibility using special rules. We are not to throw our ordinary perceptions out the window, but to employ them in certain distinctive ways. The perceptions we employ include our understanding of natural or physical laws; of the literal and figurative uses of language; of aesthetic form, consistency, and balance; of ranges of human character; of ethical imperatives, and so on. Our entire understanding of how the world works is involved. The fact that an imaginative construct may require an adjustment of ordinary assumptions in a category of understanding that is also used outside the realm of fiction-reading — such as in the understanding of natural laws — does not mean that such a category does not apply to fiction, even to non-realistic fiction.

The types of plausibility to be assessed are affected by the adjustments we have agreed to make to accommodate the particular work; e.g., when we are adjusted for fantasy, we make a different type of plausibility assessment with respect to natural and physical laws than we do when reading a realistic novel. When reading heroic literature, we make an adjustment in the assessment of plausible character that differs from the assessment of realistic literature, and so on. Accordingly, there is always a correlation between our sense of the type of fiction we are reading — its mode and genre — and our understanding of the work's meaning. We are always making decisions and choices about the text we are reading, and these decisions and choices ultimately determine what we take away from the text, the quality and level of the impact on us.

In the case of New Testament narrative which I am reading in this book, consisting of the gospels and the Acts of the Apostles, I have made decisions which affect this impact greatly, namely, the decision to read the narratives as fiction, and the decision to read them as texts largely discrete from the rest of the Bible, both Old and New Testaments. This discreteness does not mean that I ignore the Biblical context, and in fact I accept arguments which others have made that these texts are largely based on Old Testament analogues, but rather I mean that I am reading non-doctrinally: both by assuming the stories are not historical, and by not reading them as fulfillments of prophecy, and not as somehow mutually consistent when they are not. In reading non-doctrinally, of course I am reading them out of the context of their intended purpose. Therefore, some justification is in order.

Reasons to Read the Gospels as Fiction

There are good reasons to read the gospels as fiction. Indicia of fiction are obviously present in these works. In the absence of doctrinal belief, which requires the reader to construct and to impose on the Greco-Roman world a separate empirical reality from that which one normally inhabits or posits, the most obvious indicator is the use of fantasy. Even committed Christians have argued that the fantastic details of the gospels should be read as fiction, or at least not as literal fact. They argue, for example, that the virgin birth of Matthew and Luke derives from the effort to "fulfill" a prophecy from Isaiah 7:14 which was based on the Septuagint's mistranslation of the Hebrew word for a young woman.[1] Bishop Spong believes that if Biblical texts are not treated as being readable by intelligent, modern adults, Christianity will die out.[2] The purpose we have for not relinquishing the gospels to fundamentalist Christians is similar, but not the same: we hope to preserve the book. The gospels are too rich and suggestive to be abandoned to simplistic and doctrinaire readings, which is the same as marking them as off-limits to intellectuals. I see no good reason to do this.

The second indicator of fictionality is the evidence, seen in comparisons among the gospels, of the reworking of themes and episodes without regard to reliability or stability in the fact pattern, but with great emphasis placed on putting across one's lessons. We see this in the episode involving the woman who anoints Jesus, the protest against it, and the Simon or Lazarus character, which is the episode I refer to in this book as the "stopover in Bethany," appearing in the three synoptic gospels. The constantly shifting details, the shifts in characters, the alteration of a parable to an incident, and the wide variation in both meaning and event from the first version of this episode to the last, reveal beyond a doubt that the foremost urgency in the minds of the writers was not giving an accurate account of events, but rather shaping a tale for its best didactic purpose. These purposes are discussed with more detail in my final chapter, but primarily by reference to midrashic theories which are summarized without great detail, as my purpose does not require great detail. Readers who wish to study this topic may do so by referring to the cited texts. Related to this idea, in Chapters 1 and 8, is the idea of the connection between cultural survival and messianism, which in its own way provides further evidence for the allegorical nature of the gospels: the gospels thus contain a deep cultural truth, but the details of the story are invented.

A similar example of purposeful manipulation by the authors is seen in their use of characters (the disciples) who inhabit a world of free-flowing magic, and yet who at times exhibit difficulty in understanding or believing in the magical powers of the very leader they profess to follow, against the evidence of their senses. This problem can arise only from construction and invention of a fictional nature. The critic Tzvetan Todorov has described this technique of invention, which is done for the purposes of creating identification between the "hesitating" character and the reader, as the defining characteristic of fantastic literature.[3]

A third indicator of fictionality is the figurative, usually allegorical, use of language. A character whose name means "Anointed Savior" and whose role in the story exactly matches

3

that name is likely to have been invented by authors writing with an allegorical or quasi-allegorical purpose. The above-mentioned techniques all belong to fiction writers with didactic purposes, not to historians, biographers, or memoirists.

We conclude, then, that the gospels are actually a form of fiction, or are at least enough like fiction to be analyzed as fiction. The recognized genre to which the gospels belong is that of "apocalyptic literature." Therefore, that genre will receive some discussion in a later chapter.

Independent of any claim that the gospels are a form of fiction is the idea that it may be valuable to read them as fiction because doing so reveals the nature of the process of reading fiction, all the more so because the gospels are composed in an extinct genre. The difference between what was done then and what is done now throws the nature of what is done into relief: what is done when we read, what must have been expected or assumed when the writers wrote, what was possible, what is no longer possible, what is still possible.

Moreover, in contrasting these processes with those we use to assess quasi-historical narrative (the Acts), we conclude that the assessment of fiction involves evaluating the plausibility of characters and events within a framework of premises which must themselves first be accepted, whereas the quasi-historical narrative involves assessment of plausibility only or primarily in terms of whether or not the events are likely to have occurred; except, however, that fantastic history dispenses with that assessment and is akin to the adventure story or legend, something read mainly for the pleasure of its event, rather than its plausibility.

Fictional versus Historical Plausibility

Fictional plausibility assessment is similar to historical plausi-bility assessment, but is at an additional remove from the sense of empirical reality. The sense of empirical reality is involved in both assessments, but in fiction it is used (to a greater or lesser extent, depending on the taste of the reader) to test the premises, not the content. The content is assessed against the premises. (This is why it is "unrealistic" when the disciples don't believe in the miracles of Jesus — when they are "obstinate" about the loaves and fish: after repeated demonstration, why would they be? Their behavior, the content of the story, does not make sense in terms of the premises of the story.) However, in history, the premises consist of the sense of empirical reality, which is external to the story; except that this is not the case with ancient history, which routinely employs legend ("fantastic" history). To paraphrase one historian of religion, storytelling was once the stuff of history.[4] Today, historians still seek a good story, and there will always be problems with accuracy, but it is considered bad form to embellish and prevaricate. For today's historians, the concept of a "good story" no longer routinely includes the tall tale.

It is only by comparing these works one to another and by reading them in the context of our understanding of how the narrative genres operate that such rules of thumb about the nature of plausibility assessment are made possible. That, finally, is some justification for having undertaken this enterprise.

Jesus, Christ, and the Logos

One of the benefits made available to us by the work of the "historical Jesus" scholars (whom I discuss mostly in Chapter 1) is the awareness they give us that Jesus is one character or concept and the Christ is another. In the order of Christian composition, Jesus precedes the Christ, and, in turn, the Christ precedes its identification with the Logos, which is at least partly a Platonic concept. It is only doctrine that prevents us from seeing this for ourselves, for once we are aware of it we can see by reading the gospels in their probable order of composition how the idea develops.

To be sure, the concept of the Jewish messiah generally, and the "Son of Man" from the Book of Daniel (KJV 7:13; but see also NEB), precede the gospels and are incorporated into their soteriology or concepts of salvation, but Christology appears to be a Greek idea associated with the Logos. In the Christian gospels the connection to the Logos does not appear until the Gospel of John.

Greek Christology is distinct from the concept of a Jewish messiah in that it does not refer to a militaristic national or tribal savior in the political sense, but rather to a more personal savior not limited by tribal identification, and focused on spiritual, not political salvation. As has often been pointed out, these ideas were suited to the insecure and cosmopolitan nature of the Hellenized Roman Empire and were characteristic of the mystery religions then popular.[5]

The Gospel of John's identification of Jesus with the Logos transformed the story of Jesus from one about a prophet who may have been himself the prophesied savior of the Jewish people into a myth about a Greek (i.e., universal) god who was himself a divine emanation and emissary to the earth sent to save it from, and/or to condemn it for, its sin.

For literary critics, particularly those interested in so-called "theory," the concept of the Logos must be highly significant in any attempt conceptually to come to terms with the Gospel of John and/or the problem of doctrinal containment of open-minded reading of the New Testament. "Infinitist theologies are always logocentrisms," writes Derrida[6] and logocentrism means (unless I misunderstand Derrida) Logos Centrism. Western metaphysics, for those who are (or were) involved in that almost Catholic mystery known as the deconstructive enterprise, begins with the mysterious enunciation of the Divine Word and Wisdom, or Logos. This enunciation is, for deconstructionists, a conceptual error. For the record, I have done my best, in this book, not to write in TheorySpeak.

Anyway, the first section of this book has not attempted to

deal at length with this complex philosophical issue. Whether the concept of the Logos is an error, or whether it is a Greek form of theology incompatible with the tendency of modern science to objectify and dominate, as Gadamer seems to have argued (I am simplifying his ideas considerably), I cannot say. Of all the formulations and references to or explanations of the Logos that I have read, those of Gadamer come the closest to making sense to me, but the truth is that I cannot be made to understand the idea.[7] The problem is that in every such formulation, the language of the formulation clearly implies a metaphor, but the terms of the metaphor remain always abstract and often circular. Thus, for example, Gadamer writes:

> In considering the being of beings, Greek metaphysics regarded it as a being that fulfilled itself in thought. The thought is the thought of nous, which is conceived as the highest and most perfect being, gathering within itself the being of all beings. The articulation of the logos brings the structure of being into language, and this coming into language is, for Greek thought, nothing other than the presencing of the being itself, its alethia. Human thought regards the infinity of this presence as its fulfilled potential, its divinity.[8]

Gadamer considered this concept "self-forgetful," and took exception to the idea that language can have an infinite presence. On the contrary, language, and therefore also historical experience is, for Gadamer, finite. I mention this so as not to suggest that Gadamer was endorsing this definition or description of the Logos. Rather, the point is that even this relatively straightforward description is, indeed, "self-forgetful." Try to follow it: a being fulfills itself in the thought of the highest being, which contains the being of all beings, whose structure is brought into the realm of language, which becomes an infinite presence, which is divinity because it is a fulfilled potential — !

It doesn't help that the concept of generation is introduced into these circularities by speaking of a "son" or a "father," in the manner of both John's gospel and the gnostics. The Son then is a word, which is a thought, which is a presence (it is "presence" that really bedevils the deconstructionists), which is existent from the beginning of time, yet generated by the Father, and so on.

To track down such mysteries to their originary lairs would perhaps be a futile, and certainly an endless endeavor. No matter how significant, I have had to decline that endeavor. I would note, however, that those who object to the readings in this book on doctrinal grounds ought at least to acknowledge the nature of their own theology before attacking these readings on bases that they pretend are normative.

Finally, I must advise the reader that the composition of most of this book was complete in about 2003, and that it is an essay. The wise reader will know what to make of those two facts.

Chapter I

Literary Criticism & The Historical Jesus

The purpose of this first chapter is to point out three methodological errors which occur in the work of certain writer/scholars
in or on the fringes of the field of "historical Jesus" research, all
of which derive from an insufficient appreciation of the
historicity of literary criticism. I will also outline in this chapter
a view of the origins of Christian narrative myth as revealed by
an analysis of apocalyptic genre and historical context. My thesis
is that Christian narrative myth (the gospels) incorporates and to
some extent symbolizes a Jewish sect's survival response to the
destruction of Jerusalem by the Romans in 70 C.E. I do not
advance this idea with the purpose of antagonizing the devout,
but out of a genuine and long-standing interest in the nature of
the Bible as a literary artifact.

Background

For centuries, Christian intellectuals have been trying to come to
terms with, and to appropriate for their own purposes, post-
Enlightenment methods of "historical criticism." The idea has
always been to contain the threat that rose to prominence in the
Age of Reason to religious hegemony over ideas. Thus,
"historical criticism" to these intellectuals is a branch of theology
tactically aimed at containing flight from the church based on a
weakening of belief in Christian miracles and orthodoxy. It is not
really a historical method, because history, as treated in this
method, is checked by the primacy of doctrine. As Edgar Krentz
has written, "History is studied to remove it in favor of nonhistorical truth. … Theology must either justify the use of historical
criticism and define its nature or be willing to reformulate the
Christian faith in terms of a positivist truth that historicism alone

will validate." [1]

According to Krentz, historical criticism became generally accepted over time, and was made a duty for Christian intellectuals by a papal encyclical in 1943. In a large sense, the method was defined by a pontifical commission in 1964 as including "source analysis, textual criticism, literary criticism, linguistic studies, and the method of form history." Today it includes these categories and also philological study ("forms, significance, and meaning of language and literature") and redaction criticism.[2]

"Literary criticism" for Christian intellectuals means mainly ancient or classical forms. Krentz defines it as treating "the rhetorical, poetic, and compositional devices used by an author to structure his thought and embellish it with suitable language."[3] This limited definition can mislead a modern, general reader of the spate of "historical Jesus" books which appeared in the last decades of the twentieth century, because the writers of these books refer to "literary criticism" without clarifying that what they refer to is a practice that took place between the times of Aristotle and Augustine. They deny all historicity to "literary criticism" in painting a picture of it that a literary critic of today would not recognize.

If we actually apply current basic literary critical principles to Biblical texts, we can and do get historical results. Moreover, all literary criticism contains certain historicist principles, and some literary criticism is overtly historicist. That said, we will proceed to:

Error No. 1: Literary Criticism is Ahistorical

In volume 1 of his book, *A Marginal Jew,* John P. Meier states flatly that "literary criticism" is "an ahistorical approach" to documents with truth claims for which people were willing to die.[4] As valuable as literary criticism is for certain purposes, it doesn't deal with truth claims — doesn't validate or invalidate them. The idea appears to be that literary criticism never intersects with either the "real" world or the "historical" detail. The "real" and the "historical" are seen as distinct from each other, but both are equally inaccessible to the literary critic. Meier thus concludes that literary criticism "cannot be the main method in a quest for the historical Jesus."[5]

"Quest" is an interesting word. It was the word Albert Schweitzer used. [6] Schweitzer ended his book by abandoning history in favor of ineffable mystery, along the lines of the "removal" in favor of nonhistorical truth described by Krentz above.[7] Notwithstanding such abandonments, to go on a quest for something means that we seek it; we hope to find it; it is our most cherished goal, like the quest for the Holy Grail. Such an undertaking is entirely different from one in which we seek to ascertain whether or not materials exist which would support a finding that Jesus had an historical existence, and which we would then use to determine the extent and nature of this historical existence. It is true that a post-Enlightenment literary criticism should not assume historicity without evidence; but then, what intellectual discipline should assume it? With respect to the Jesus stories, it is only the theology of orthodox Christianity which asks us to assume the historicity of Jesus, whereas both history and literary criticism should require that we first examine the materials before we determine the nature of the quest. Our history may turn out to be a history of theology; our literary study may turn out to be the formal (or historical) study of a myth, a legend, or a midrashic liturgical composition. So if "quest" has a tendentious burden, then indeed, literary criticism cannot be the "main method" in the quest, since it does not assume the result. But neither can "historical criticism" be the main method, unless it is defined (and Krentz essentially defines it this way) as subserving the needs of theology.

Not surprisingly, Meier defines his form of "historical criticism" in exactly this subservient way. His confession of theological purpose is stated as follows:[8]

[T]he proper object of Christian faith is not and cannot be an idea or scholarly reconstruction, however reliable. What, then is the usefulness of the historical Jesus to people of faith? My reply is: none [for religious purposes]. Yet, I maintain that the quest can be very useful if one is asking about theology, in a contemporary context. [O]nce a culture becomes permeated with a historical-critical approach, as has Western culture from the Enlightenment onward, theology can operate in and speak to that culture with credibility only if it absorbs into its methodology a historical approach.

Thus, the purpose of the "quest for the historical Jesus" is to increase credibility for theology in a post-Enlightenment culture. Such a purpose is patently ahistorical. And yet *literary criticism* is dismissed as incapable of being the "main method" in the "quest" because *it* is supposedly ahistorical.

As it turns out, the confession of theological purpose occurs in more than one work to be discussed in this book, and is a more or less conscious apology offered usually deep into the text. Where it is not openly confessed, it appears as a sudden, inexplicable inconsistency in the logic of one's method. We shall see further examples later on. Here, it is worth paraphrasing Meier's remarks distinguishing the "real" from the "historical." The historian has, essentially, two difficulties: determining what is "real," and determining what is "historical." The historian has the same problem in knowing anything about the "real" Jesus as he has about knowing the "real" Nixon or Reagan, and the same problem in knowing anything about the "historical" Jesus that he has in knowing anything about the "historical" Thales, or the "historical" Apollonius of Tyana.[9] On the one hand, knowledge of history is not the same as knowledge of the real, since history is a theoretical construct based on available materials. We can get closer to the "real" Nixon than to the "real" Thales, because we have a great deal of available material on Nixon, consisting of his own writings, contemporary accounts, news stories, memoirs, film and videotape, presidential archives, and so on, whereas all we know of Thales comes from references to him and to his ideas in a few ancient works by other writers, such as Aristotle and Diogenes Laertius.[10] (Copleston, Chapter 3.1). But the "real" Nixon still eludes us, and what we have are various "historical" Nixons, being the interpretations of various historians. This homage to postmodern relativism is fair enough, as far as it goes. But, writes Meier, "the difficulty of knowing anything about Jesus must be placed in the larger context of the difficulty of knowing anything about Thales, Apollonius of Tyana, or anyone else in the ancient world" (24). We are much less able to construct a "historical" Thales or a "historical" Jesus, because the materials on each, as on most ancient figures, are so limited.

Notice how the argument operates. Step 1: The "real" is more difficult than the "historical" and is essentially unknowable: *as with Jesus, so with Nixon*. Step 2: The "historical" becomes more difficult to assess insofar as the subject is more remote in time: *as with Jesus, so with Thales*. An implication exists in the double comparison, which is that Jesus is *as real as Nixon* and *as historical as Thales*, but the explicit point is that there is less "reality" data on Jesus than on Nixon, and as meager "historical" data on Jesus as on Thales. We note that what we might consider the "first question" of any book purporting to deal with the issue of a "historical Jesus" — the question of whether or not Jesus existed — is being set up to go begging. "Reality" is impossible, and "history" is impossibly difficult, so we are to assume both, *as we do with Nixon and Thales*.

Let's focus more specifically on the implication that Jesus is *as* "historical" as Thales, and that the historical data on each is equally meager. Generally stated, the idea is that all ancient figures are difficult to document, and they all occupy an equally difficult "historical" status. This equation of the historical Thales with the historical Jesus is both imprecise and misleading, and it overlooks a principle of literary criticism which would require a distinction between the two figures. The equation is imprecise because *the type of literature we have about Jesus is qualitatively different from the type of literature we have about Thales.* It is misleading because it places Jesus at the same level of historicity as Thales — whereas an impartial examination of the evidence, which accounts for the differences in the quality of the literature on each figure, may not place them at the same level of verifiable historicity at all. The principle of literary criticism which we would apply is one that was most famously applied over half a century ago by Northrop Frye in *Anatomy of Criticism,* which is that we compare literary works with one another.[11] We then distinguish between them and account for their differences. If we apply that principle to the works that turn out to be — consistent with Meier's discussions and implications — the primary sources of information about our two figures, i.e., the New Testament canon and, say, the life of Thales by Diogenes Laertius,[12] we understand that these works are not even remotely similar in nature or known purpose.

Obviously, the gospels are full of miracles, which are offered to the reader in the spirit of willingness to believe. Thus, water-into-wine, loaves-and-fishes, calming the storm, walking on water, transfiguration, faith healings, resurrections from the dead, ascensions to heaven, etc. These stories are known to all of us with a Christian background, whereas fewer people will have read Diogenes Laertius. Without making any claims for the accuracy of the fact recital in Diogenes, its facts are obviously of a different nature than the gospel "facts," and are offered in a different spirit and manner. There are no miracles in Diogenes. Instead, we learn such things as the names of Thales' parents, the probable places of his origin, the names of his treatises on astronomy, his basic philosophical doctrines, his discoveries and experiments (e.g., he measures the height of the pyramids by measuring their shadow at the hour when our shadow is the same length as ourselves), and so on; and the consistent method of Diogenes is to reveal sources of his information: Plato, Aristotle, Hippias, Pamphila, Hieronymus, Eleusis, Alexo, Hermippus — there are dozens of them (Diogenes I:23-35 & passim). While most of the sources cannot today be checked because they have been lost, the technique of attribution is routinely followed in a manner similar to the manner of scholarship up to the present day. The scholar does not assume or require belief on his own say-so, and he provides his materials for the reader who wishes to verify or conduct his or her own research. Only Luke among the evangelists uses language even remotely resembling the language of attribution, and then only in the opening chapter:

> The author to Theophilus: Many writers have undertaken to draw up an account of the events that have happened among us, following the traditions handed down to us by the original eyewitnesses and servants of the Gospel. (Lk. 1:1-2, NEB).

Even in Luke the language of narration is much more like the language typically associated with storytelling: "In the days of Herod, king of Judea, there was a priest named Zechariah ... " (Lk. 1:5 NEB). And even Luke's "eyewitnesses" appear to be eyewitnesses to something that may or may not refer to events: thus "eyewitnesses and servants *of the Gospel,*" in the NEB, and "eyewitnesses and ministers *of the word*" in the ASV (Lk. 1:2, italics added). Today's literary critic would immediately recognize and consider significant the fact that the gospels on the one hand, and Diogenes' life of Thales on the other, are two entirely different types of works, the nature of which leads us to different conclusions about the reliability of the "facts" each gives us. It is ironic that Meier gives lip service to a version of this principle without applying it to the texts in question, when he writes:

> [C]ontemporary literary criticism provides a salutary caveat
> by reminding us to ask what is the literary function of a verse
> or pericope in the larger work before we glibly declare it a
> reliable source of historical information (12).

Meier thus wants to limit the role of the literary critic to
perceiving parts within wholes, while not commenting on differences between wholes, but he does concede here that the
perception of function has a relationship to an analysis of what
constitutes historical "fact." Unfortunately, this scrap is thrown
out as a professional courtesy only, for there is to be no recognition that literary function has anything at all to say in determining what is or is not historical fact. And this is fine, insofar as
Meier is not claiming to practice literary criticism. But what is
less acceptable is that this dismissal, like the mistaken equations
of Nixon/Thales/Jesus, is merely part of a well-worn pattern in
which a quasi-historical methodology serves the ends of
theology.

This pattern typically begins by pointing out the paucity of
historical materials — the limitations of Tacitus, of the
bowdlerized, "Slavonic" Josephus, of the agrapha or unwritten
sayings and deeds, of the apocryphal gospels (above all, those) —
and then concludes, inevitably:

> The four canonical gospels turn out to be the only large
> documents containing significant blocks of material relevant
> to a quest for the historical Jesus (Meier 139).

This will always be the conclusion of those who pretend an
interest in historicity, but whose interest is in fact doctrinal. Thus,
we can go back to a rather dated handbook by John H. Hayes,
called *Introduction to the Bible* and find much the same thing:

> This survey of the non-Biblical and non-Gospel material

mentioning Jesus shows that, in the last analysis, an attempted portrayal of the Jesus of history must be dependent upon the New Testament Gospels (323).

And what has been the logical process by which Hayes has rejected his "non-Gospel" sources? As to the apocryphal gospels, it includes quoting from passages in which the infant Jesus creates twelve sparrows out of clay, then claps his hands causing them to fly away chirping; or in which father Joseph is building a bed for a rich man and finds that he has two beams of uneven size, whereupon infant Jesus magically stretches them to an equal size. "This material," writes our analyst, "is obviously the product of a pious and devout Christian imagination, but it contains no semblance of historical actuality and *can thus be dismissed as a valid source of information* on the historical Jesus" (Hayes 322, italics added.) It hardly need be pointed out that the canonical gospels contain material no less miraculous, and that the description given above fits them equally well — and yet *they* are not to be wholeheartedly "dismissed as a valid source of information." In this case, it is not a matter of failing to distinguish between different types of works, but rather of creating a false distinction between types of works (the apocryphal and canonical gospels) that are in the most obvious and significant way similar. One could no doubt find distinctions between them, but the distinction cannot be found in focusing on the nature of a miraculous event. If such events invalidate a source of information, they must invalidate both sources.

There are thus two types of historicity recognized by literary criticism which are ignored by the approaches of these writers. One is the level of historicity associated with types of literary texts, that is, history of genre. What Todorov has said about Roman Jakobson's theory of genres could be said here, although Jakobson's application is different:

The types of discourse, traditionally called genres, are formed, according to Jakobson, around the expansion of certain verbal categories (Todorov, TOTS 281).[13]

A text that begins, "In the time of King So-and-So, there was a priest named Such-and-Such" is language within a narrative tradition which the literary critic recognizes as what we might call the "Once Upon a Time" tradition; a history could conceivably begin this way, but much more common following language like this comes a fairy tale, or certainly something both traditional and fictitious. A random examination of the opening passages of the Grimms' fairytales demonstrates the technique [14]:

A long, long while ago there was a King ...
("The Golden Bird")

In Switzerland there lived an old Count, who had an only son. ...
("The Three Languages")

Once upon a time there was a King's son, who had a mind to see the world. ... ("The Riddle")

Once again, here is Luke:

In the days of Herod, king of Judea, there happened to be this priest named Zechariah ... (1:5 ASV)

Or we might compare the language of etiological myth to the famous opening lines of the Gospel of John. Here are some etiological myth examples, and we include Genesis over the anticipated objections:

First of all, the Void came into being, next broad-bosomed Earth, the solid and eternal home of all ... (Hesiod, Theogony II:116ff.)

There was in the very beginning nothing whatever. There was no sky, no earth, no water, but just empty space. (Juaneño/Luiseño myth) (Gifford 102)

In the beginning of creation, when God made heaven and earth, the earth was without form and void ... (Genesis 1:1-2, NEB)

This is the beginning of the Ancient Word, here in this place called Quiché. Here we shall inscribe, we shall implant the Ancient Word, the potential and source for everything done in the citadel of Quiché, in the nation of the Quiché people. (Popol Vuh) (Tedlock 71).

And, of course, John:

In the beginning there was the divine word and wisdom. (1:1 ASV)

In the beginning was the Word. ... (1:1 NKJV)

By contrast, and having no etiological function at all, the *Life of Thales* begins:

Herodotus, Duris, and Democritus are agreed that Thales was the son of Examyas and Cleobulina, and belonged to the Thelidae, who are Phoenicians ... (Diogenes I:22).

One might perhaps argue that the parentage information in Diogenes compares more aptly to the genealogies in Matthew or

Luke, but Luke traces the genealogy to God, and both Matthew and Luke are preserving a tradition of the savior's Davidic descent, whereas no such theologoumenic principle governs the parentage and home-town information in Diogenes. Obviously, my point is that there is sufficient patterning in the language examples above (allowing for translation, and obviously making no claims of influence, since the Biblical texts are likely the oldest) to indicate a genre, or quasi-genre, thus enabling the comparison of literary wholes which Meier and others neglect to acknowledge as a function of literary criticism. A literary whole such as a genre is, in turn, defined, in part, by its relationship to certain types of distinctions we make between what is fictive or non-fictive, or "real" and "unreal." This point will be developed at greater length further on, but we may observe at this juncture that a fairy tale is a highly fictive form, as is an etiological myth, whereas a life history is less so.

The second type of historicity with which literary criticism must necessarily deal, whether or not one accepts its philosophical premises, is the historicity associated with so-called "imitation of reality."[15] There is a history of mimetic analysis going back to Aristotle, and it is based on what we, from our post-Enlightenment perspective, might call the sense of an empirically stable reality. Aristotle distinguishes between artistic imitations of men "either as better than in real life, or as worse, or as they are" (Aristotle II). This "as they are," while not exactly a concept of realism (it refers to relative moral qualities), is at least an empirically stable norm against which variations are assessed. We may or may not accept Hume's assessment of miracles, which allows us to judge of their plausibility from bases in our own experience. However, it would be an oversimplification to suggest that the notion of an empirically stable reality is an Enlightenment concept foreign to the ancient world, because, Aristotle aside, the ancient world's very perception of a miracle depends on it. Something which broke all the rules of nature might be seen, in the ancient world, as an invitation to believe in a supernatural deity who was breaking these rules, whereas after the Enlightenment, these rules became natural "laws," the breaking of which would be more likely to invite disbelief. However, the rules or "laws" were the same ones, or else there would be no ancient perception of the miraculous. As we have seen, the scholars of religion use such a concept of an empirically stable norm (viz., the clay sparrows), but only selectively, while at the same time denying that the concept is available to literary critics, who — so they imagine — deal with neither history nor reality. Such an arbitrary use of the concept of an empirically stable reality is without logical foundation.

Another religiously-trained writer who considers literary criticism to be an ahistorical discipline is Jack Miles, who claims to be writing it. Miles opposes the "historical Jesus" school. It is precisely the supposed ahistoricity of literary criticism that attracts Miles. "Literary appreciation," he writes, "cultivates internal references, made for their aesthetic effect, by preference to external references valuable for their historical information" (262). The exegete who is free from noticing the similarities between the Christ cult and contemporary Greco-Roman mystery religions is freed from what Miles calls "seeing through the Bible," something he is very much against. "A work of literary art is like a stained-glass window: It exists essentially not to be seen through but to be looked at." But historical New Testament criticism "labors endlessly to see through it. ... Why take so narrowly instrumental an attitude toward a work of the imagination?" (Miles 265).

The notion of literary criticism which Miles has naïvely adopted here as universal is one that literary critics would recognize as a theory of autotelic literature. Again, Todorov's cataloguing of symbolist theories is useful here, but it is clear from reading it that autotelism is only one theory of one mode of literature. For example, Schelling is said to have distinguished between symbolism and allegory on the basis that symbolism was autotelic and allegory heterotelic (Todorov TOTS 209). Todorov writes that both Novalis and Sartre saw poetry as, or desired that it should be, pure autotelism (TOTS 275). But if we can distinguish a genre that is heterotelic (referring to something outside itself) then we have established a realm of literature beyond the autotelic. Moreover, Todorov's discussion of the autotelic function of symbolism is fairly well confined to the French symbolist movement, because that is where the theory and practice of autotelism is most often found. One thinks preeminently of Mallarmé, who is really difficult or impossible to "see through" in the way Miles finds so objectionable.

The disingenuousness or perhaps the naiveté of Miles' type of quixotism is suggested by the simile he employs to illustrate it. Literary critics are not people who stare mindlessly at stained glass windows while historical critics look through the colored glass at objects beyond them. The critical mind, whether historical or literary, does not "see through" so much as it sees *in*. The stained glass window does not exist merely to be stared at, but to be contemplated. It has a function and, in many cases, a narrative content. There are stained glass windows which depict scenes from the Bible, others which merely present skillful geometric designs. We are interested in the scenes depicted, in the materials used, in the artists who made the windows, above all in the tradition of such windows, as perhaps also in the tradition of different types of windows for comparative purposes. But all seeing *in* for Miles is a seeing *through,* and subsections in his appendices are entitled "How Not to See Through the Bible" and "Learning how not to see through the Bible" (Miles 265, 274).

The supposed ahistoricity of literary criticism leads directly to the second methodological error, which is a confusion about the source of one's assumptions. We shall describe this error as:

Error No. 2: Confusing Doctrine with Literary Criticism when Defining One's Text

The basis for Miles's sense of urgency about not "seeing through the Bible" is not literary but religious, and the method used by Miles is demonstrably *not* literary. It is based on a definition of the text provided by the patristic fathers of the Church: to wit, the text is The Bible. In *Christ,* Miles offers his views of Jesus as a character who appears in a text that is defined as beginning with Genesis and ending with the Book of Revelation. With complete accuracy, he explains that

> ... the belief appropriated or transposed here has been the classic Christian belief that 'Jesus is Lord' (Rom. 10:9) — the dogma, foreshadowed in the NT and formally defined at the first ecumenical councils, that Jesus Christ was and is God Incarnate ... (Miles 248).

Thus, for Miles, Jesus equals Yahweh, and so his book explores the psychodrama of how and why God "changed his mind" so much during that millennium-plus stretch of time between the story about Adam and the story about Jesus. What is both obvious and utterly un-literary-critical is precisely this definition of the text, which is purely doctrinal. It is a definition rejected by everyone other than the ecumenical councils Miles refers to and the believing Christians who follow their lead. It is also, quite clearly, an ahistorical definition, unless one accepts the position that the writer(s) of Genesis and Exodus knew that their works prefigured the Gospels to be written centuries later — or unless one accepts the Calvinist type ultra-simplification of the doctrinal position, which is that "God" "wrote" the (Christian) Bible.

In literary-critical studies, definition of the text is an obvious first step, but critics seldom spend much time on it, because in most cases the text is readily defined. I am not speaking now about subtexts and undertexts and material bases and all the jargon and subtlety of the deconstructive enterprise, but rather the simple question, "Which work are we studying?" In all of the literary critical studies I have read or am able to conceive of, the answer to this question is historically determined, meaning that it is a matter of record. We are studying Chaucer's *Canterbury Tales,* Shakespeare's *Julius Caesar,* Twain's *Adventures of Huckleberry Finn,* because, aside from being worth studying, they are discrete compositions, so designed by their authors and so understood by their readers. Or perhaps we are studying The Nun's Priest's Tale, or the last act of *Julius Caesar,* or the first two thirds of *Huckleberry Finn.* In the first instance, the definition of the text arises from the act of the author (composition), in the second instance from the acts of both author and critic (composition and functionally meaningful selection). In both cases, definition of the text is related to form: we are studying, in the above examples as initially defined, (1) a collection of explicitly interrelated or, specifically, "framed" tales; (2) a tragic history play; (3) a novel: the three definitions so designed by the authors of the works. In the second set of definitions, we are studying: (1) a single tale from the collection; (2) a single act from the play; (3) a structural segment of the novel: the three definitions so understood or designated by their reader-critics. The second type of definition adds function to the historical act of an author, but even if there were no known author, function (more specifically, the perception of a structural whole) would define the text and imply the historical act of its having been composed. We don't know who the Bible's authors were, but we perceive that Genesis is a text distinct from the Gospel of Luke, and this is a historical as well as a functional perception.

There are times, and they are not common, when works which are complete and self-contained are considered within a definition that includes other complete and self-contained works: for example, in examination of trilogies, tetralogies, or poem-sequences. Thus, *The Divine Comedy* is the name for that defin-ition of a text which includes its three constituent narrative poems; or Shakespeare's sonnets may be read as a sequence containing two or three major themes which allow the sonnets to comment on one another, or to demonstrate development of the themes and to provoke speculation on the personal relationships indicated (in itself an external reference and a historical concern). But I can think of no examples in which the definition of a text would include works by different authors who were not by their own intention co-authors of a given work. One may widen the scope of one's study as much as one likes, but then one is discussing a variety of texts, not a single text actually authored by a number of people, as is required by the Christian doctrinal definition of the text as "The Bible." Reasonable Christians do admit that "The Bible," although a single book, is actually a collection of texts.

Postmodern critics despise all normative concepts, but I think I can slip one in here without arousing too much odium, since its purpose is quite limited. Most people who practice literary criticism would admit that the tendency of most literary criticism is toward discreteness of definition. It would very much surprise me to read a study of Joyce's *Stephen Hero,* an early draft of *Portrait of the Artist as a Young Man,* and not to find the critic carefully distinguishing the Stephen of *this* text from the Stephen of *that other* text. And yet the definition of text that Miles wants us to accept is one that lumps together as one conceptual whole a variety of tales, tribal laws, prophecies, proverbs, poems, and visions that were authored in different languages and countries by authors who lived as temporally removed from one another as twelve hundred years or more. Aside from Miles's admission that this textual definition is doctrinal, it is obviously *not* literary, because it follows neither history nor function.

Like Meier, Miles makes it quite clear that his approach is governed by theological concerns. In objecting to historical criticism, Miles complains that it "dissolves the dynamic tension of monotheism by tracing different character traits to different ancient sources" so that "the character himself [i.e., God] is gone, dissolved into a polytheism of component parts" (Miles 248). He claims that in his own book God is seen "neither as the object of religious belief nor as a topic in ancient history but as the central character in a work of literature" (248). But there can be only one reason why that "central character" does not involve us in a necessary discussion of Milton, Dante, and Spenser, and that answer is found in the decision of the first ecumenical councils. The reason it is to be found there is that only by finding it there can one preserve monotheism. So we are to ignore such historical facts as the passage of twelve hundred years, the displacement of civilizations, the apparent changes in the nature of Jewish theology; and we assert that this ahistoricity is the result of — not Christian doctrine (even though we admit that our conceptual position derives from it), but the *practice of literary criticism*. Such a conclusion is without logic.

The third methodological error we shall discuss derives from, and will be referred to as:

Error No. 3: Failing to Recognize the Full Implications of the Historicity Inherent in Form

This third methodological error goes beyond simply misunderstanding the nature of "literary criticism" and includes the failure to grasp necessary relationships between history and literary form. It is less an error of commission than one of degree. In the two works I wish to complain of — and they are both interesting and valuable works — the authors do recognize that the form of a work reveals historical data; or, to put it more precisely, that form and history reveal one another because they are interrelated. In both cases, however, the implications toward which these works lead in their analysis of this interrelation fade into invisibility just at the point where they should leap into relief.

The first book that falls into this error is Bishop John S. Spong's *Liberating the Gospels*, which is based in large measure on the scholarly work of M.D. Goulder. Following Goulder's lead, Spong essentially recognizes through an analysis of form that the stories in the gospels are myths, legends, fairy tales. The form that is recognized is liturgical: the need was to create, within the framework of the new messianic sect within Judaism, lectionary material for the round of yearly Jewish festivals and religious observances which would replace readings from the Jewish scriptures (i.e., the "Old Testament").

According to this theory, a reading from those earlier sources which would have occurred at a certain time in the liturgical calendar is replaced by a gospel reading which closely fits that same liturgical or calendric occasion and resembles its forerunner in its themes and details. It follows, then, that the events of the gospels have a literary origin, but little or no historical basis in fact. (Spong makes an exception for the crucifixion of Jesus, which will not be addressed here.) Thus, the Sermon on the Mount is patterned on the receipt of the Ten Commandments on Mount Sinai by Moses; the miracle of the loaves and fishes is patterned after the miracle of manna in the wilderness, or after Elijah's miracle of the jar of flour (1 Kg 17:11-15); the raising of Jairus' daughter draws its inspiration from Elijah's raising of a dead child (1 Kg 17:21-24); the ascension of Jesus to heaven is patterned on a similar ascension by Elijah (2 Kg 2:11); Matthew's account of Herod's death decree for male Jewish babies and the escape to Egypt re-tells the perils of the infant Moses in Exodus 1 — and so on.[16] Because of the number and closeness of the literary parallels, it becomes obvious, completely aside from all considerations of empirically stable reality, that the events of the gospels are ahistorical inventions; in short, fiction. Form reveals (degree of) historicity. On the other hand, it is knowledge of certain historical facts which helps us to understand the form: knowledge of the liturgical calendar, of the dates at which Christians separated off from Judaism (ca. 88 C.E.), knowledge of the earlier literature and how it was used as lectionary material in the calendar, etc.

The error I complain of here lies in failing to continue connecting the dots between history and form — between, say, Josephus and the Gospel of Luke. It is in failing to see that there is yet more corroborating evidence for the nature of the myth in the history we have, and more corroborating evidence in the myth for a history consistent with our (or Spong's) conclusions thus far. The crucial question to ask is this: If the gospels are liturgical inventions created to replicate, amplify, or replace Second Temple era Jewish lections, what was the motivation to create them? What need existed, *of which we have corroborating evidence,* for the midrashic invention at this point in Jewish history? Spong seems to suggest, based on intuition, that it was some power in the personality of Jesus that motivated all this effort, but we have better evidence available to us than intuition.

The answer is found in the *Jewish War* of Josephus and in the gospels. The motivation to create the gospels acted in conjunction with the theological needs of the new Jewish sect; the motivation included the need, somehow, to survive the impending cultural destruction of the Jews. It was the Jews who were crucified — literally, and in large numbers. The *Jewish War* is full of tales of thousands upon thousands killed and piled on one another in the streets of Jerusalem, and of crucifixions ad nauseam. In V:446-451, Josephus describes how Titus would crucify Jews outside the city walls as a terror tactic: "and so great was their number, that space could not be found for the crosses nor crosses for the bodies." It was the Jews, collectively, whose life and culture must be found to have some meaning which, to paraphrase Spong, "death could not be found to contain." (See Spong *LTG* 302, 309, and the quotations further on). It was the Roman oppression of the Jewish culture and the eventual obliteration of Jerusalem in 70 C.E. that is corroborated in history, which is transparently alluded to in the gospels, and which is suggested in the character called Jesus (Matt. 1:21: "He will save his people from their sins," ASV; "Saviour," NEB) who mirrors the Suffering Servant of Isaiah chapter 53. Jesus is a midrashic creation by a culture under siege, meant to embody and idealize that culture, and to stand for the holy and immortal one who triumphs in and through his own persecution and death. Whether or not the Jesus of the gospels was "based" on a real person is not determinable, but the character who appears in the gospels is demonstrably a literary creation — by anyone's historical theory — because all the things he does in the story are made up from preexisting theological material for theological and cultural purposes. The destruction of Jewish culture and the slaughter of Jewish people, however, was *not* made up. These two premises are accepted by proponents of the midrashic theory of gospel composition, but only the first one is given any significance.

In addition to the historical corroboration for the fact that it was the Jews, collectively, who were crucified, who suffered and died, and who rose again in a different form (as Christians), there is literary and midrashic evidence for the allegorical technique used to represent this historical fact. In Exodus 4:22, God speaks, saying: "Israel is my first-born son." As Goulder observes, the Gospel of Matthew recognizes this tradition and virtually equates Jesus with the new Israel by referring to a fulfilled prophecy: "Out of Egypt I called my son" (Matt. 2:15; cf. Hosea 11:1). "Israel was God's son in the prefiguring language of the O.T.: and it is in connection with the Exodus that he is so called" (Goulder 239.)[17]

Spong, writing for a popular audience, acknowledges that the "Man of Sorrows" sung of in Handel's Messiah, and whom Christians typically associate with Jesus, is not to be found in the gospels, but rather in the Book of Isaiah, where he is the Suffering Servant who symbolizes the people of Israel. Spong reflects on this image thus:

I suspect that this post-Exilic prophet developed this symbol so that he could help the defeated Jewish nation understand that their future did not lie in grandeur, power, or glory. ...

Luke ... intermingled the story of Jesus with the story of the servant figure of Isaiah on a fairly constant basis (LTG 251).

The obvious inference to be drawn from this intermingling is that Jesus and the Suffering Servant/Man of Sorrows represent the same thing in the gospel's collection of derivative and made-up incidents: the people of Israel, who were being crucified. On one level, it is amazing to me that Spong does not draw the inference. A literary critic dealing with this type of parallelism in any other two works would draw it. He apparently does not draw it because, like Meier and Miles, to do so would conflict with his ultimately theological purposes, admitted in such passages as these:

I cannot conceive of a way that would lead me to dismiss [Jesus'] historicity.

[Secularism will not] satisfy the deep spiritual yearnings that continue to burn inside the hearts of those hopelessly religious creatures we call Homo sapiens. So we must seek some other alternative. ... (Spong LTG 326, 284).

It is both understandable and fitting that an Episcopal bishop should have such sentiments, but theological purposes are not compatible with post-Enlightenment historical purposes. They act (because they must) as a check against an open mind.

Another type of corroboration for the inference that should be drawn is available to us in the fact that Messianism as a cultural survival tactic is attested to as recently as 1889, when the Lakota people on our own continent were threatened with extinction. The following passage, from the well known account in John G.

Neihardt's *Black Elk Speaks,* demonstrates the same sort of collective, cultural need and motivation described by Spong, Josephus, and other writers who describe or acknowledge the effect of the Jewish War on the First Century Jews. The emphasis on belief is reminiscent of the emphasis in the Gospel of John on the need to believe in order to achieve salvation through the Messiah, and the eschatological details are so similar that there was no doubt a Christian influence:

> There was a big meeting ... but I did not go over there to hear, because I did not yet believe. I thought maybe it was only the despair that made people believe, just as a man who is starving may dream of plenty of everything good to eat. I did not go over to the meeting, but I heard all they had to tell. These three men all said the same thing, and they were good men. They said that they traveled far until they came to a great flat valley near the last great mountains before the big water, and there they saw the Wanekia ["One Who Makes Live"], who was the son of the Great Spirit, and they talked to him. Wasichus [white people] called him Jack Wilson, but his name was Wovoka. He told them that there was another world coming, just like a cloud. It would come in a whirlwind out of the west and would crush out everything on this world, which was old and dying. In that other world there was plenty of meat, just like old times; and in that world all the dead Indians were alive, and all the bison that had ever been killed were roaming around again (Neihardt 236-37).

The writing of Bishop Spong on the subject of the Jewish War and Messianism is striking, precisely because it seems to recognize the connection between the two, while stopping short of the obvious conclusion. Thus, the following passage:

[The destruction of Jerusalem in 70 C.E.] changed the face of human history far more dramatically than historians have yet imagined. ... Indeed, one cannot understand the books of the New Testament unless one understands the violent history of that part of the world in which the Christian movement was first born and against which it was defined (Spong LTG 39-40).

A little further on, Spong states that survival was the only issue, and Scriptures were the weapon (LTG 45). In understanding New Testament Anti-Semitism, he writes that "each gospel inevitably reflected either that war or the tensions of anti-Jewish sentiment that followed that war's conclusion" — which explains Judas Iscariot as an invented character (LTG 274). Psychologically, the followers of Jesus sought "to lift the darkness, to ease their sense of defeat and loss" (LTG 301). This sounds exactly like what Black Elk describes, but we might recognize that in both cases, the historical defeat and loss belonged to a culture facing its own demise, not to individuals facing the loss of another individual.

Again, writing of Easter, Spong says, with a disheartening obliquity:

Some tremendous and powerful moment it must have been to force all of these symbols to gather around this life (LTG 302).

On the same page, he acknowledges that the vision of the resurrected Jesus "was not of a resuscitated body emerging from a tomb, but that was the only way they could narrate their conviction that death could not contain him."

Just so. And just as the "him" does not refer to a person rising from a grave, so it does not refer to a particular historical person confined to one, but rather to an entire society condemned to masses of graves, and symbolically represented in the most efficient way it could be narrated for liturgical purposes: by creating a midrashic character named "Savior," or, as we might say, "One Who Makes Live."

My earlier mention of the Gospel of Luke refers to the gospel's internal references to something outside itself (heterotelic function) which help to reveal its genre as a work of Jewish apocalyptic prophecy in the manner of the Book of Daniel. The references are to the coming war with Rome, and they occur in Lk. 12:49-53: "I came to set the earth on fire ... ;" 21:23, 23:28-30 (congratulations to the sterile); 21:6 (toppling of the stones of the temple); 21:20 (massing of the armies at the gates of Jerusalem); 21:24-27: " ... They will fall by the edge of the sword. ... "; 17:33-37 (sudden disappearances and murders, vultures and carcasses, etc.).[18] When read doctrinally, these passages refer to Jesus' own death and some imaginary "end time" which remains, for modern fundamentalist believers, in the indefinite future. But the form of this literature (Jewish apocalyptic prophecy) was one that relied on the contemporary historical knowledge of its readers; when read with that historical knowledge, these passages refer both to Jesus' own death and the catastrophe of the war with the Romans including the destruction of Jerusalem. Thus, a proper understanding of literary form gives us a historical meaning. This last point will be discussed in connection with the final work I wish to complain of (a little here, and more in a later chapter), A.N. Wilson's lively "biography" entitled *Paul: The Mind of the Apostle*, because the apocalyptic form is applicable to an understanding of what I consider to be errors in both his and Bishop Spong's books.

We must first define apocalyptic literature. Here is a brief description of that genre by Antonía Tripolitis, the author of a book on religions of the Hellenistic-Roman age. The italicizations are mine, indicating points that I shall emphasize:

Jewish apocalyptic literature flourished and enjoyed an enormous popularity both within Palestine and the Diaspora between 200 B.C.E. and 90 C.E. ... The apocalypticists continued the tradition of the prophets by adopting the major themes of the prophetic teachings, *in particular the prediction element,* and incorporated them into a novel world-historical, *cosmic form.* Many apocalyptic works were written during times of hardship and oppression. These conditions were depicted by the writers *in a cosmic setting, perceived not only as a local or national situation but one of universal significance,* and accompanied by supernatural signs. ... (Tripolitis 69-70).

It is quite clear to students of the gospels that they are written in "the tradition of the prophets," for there are many allusions and parallels to the books of prophecy. The more famous ones include the direct echo of Isaiah 40:3 in the opening scene of the Gospel of Mark, the Suffering Servant image already mentioned, or the virgin birth in Matthew and Luke, which is famously believed to have originated in the Septuagint's mistranslation of the word for a young girl used in Isaiah 7:14,[19]. However, the important prophetic precursor for the "prediction element" I am here focusing on is found in another direct allusion to another book of prophecy, namely the reference to the Book of Daniel in Matthew 24:15. This verse begins:

> "So when you see the 'devastating desecration' (as described by Daniel the prophet) standing 'in the holy place' (the reader had better figure out what this means), then the people in Judea should head for the hills ..."

The passage continues for some length and consists entirely of "the prediction element." Matthew 24:30 again alludes to Daniel, this time indirectly, but famously, with the image of the Son of Man coming on the clouds, which of course hearkens back to Daniel 7:13: " ... I saw one like a man coming with the clouds of heaven" (NEB). The passages are quite similar, and the debt is acknowledged. What is even more important to realize is that both books operate the same way, namely, by means of three chronological points of reference: call them A, B, and C. Point A is the time in which the book is set. Point B is the time of the predicted event, which is not named, but is known to the book's readers. It is known to them because Point C, the time of the book's composition, occurs after both Points A and B, and shortly after B — within a generation of it at most.

To characterize the three chronological points further: Point A is a historical time implanted with a fictional event, namely the prophecy. Point B is the time of a historical event known to everyone in Point C, and because of that knowledge, as well as for aesthetic, political, or theological reasons, left ambiguous. This is the "cosmic significance" that Tripolitis refers to; a direct, topical allusion would not carry cosmic significance, but topical allusion is unnecessary in any case, because of the reader's certain knowledge. Point C is unnamed; it is contemporary with the book's first readers, who carry a recent historical memory of Point B. It is essential to realize (and the error occurs precisely in *not* realizing) that the knowledge of Point B from the vantage of Point C is inescapable. This is how apocalyptic literature works. It is how Daniel worked, and it is how the gospels were meant to work. I will explain how we know this, once I have complained about Wilson's treatment of this issue.

In Wilson's book on the apostle Paul, he effectively acknowledges that the Book of Daniel operates with three chronological points of reference, as described above. More specifically, he endorses the idea that the Book of Daniel's predictions of a desecration or abomination, i.e., the profanation of the temple by idolaters, which is associated with the phrase "abomination of desolation" (See Dan. 8:13, 9:27, and especially 11:31 and 12:11), constitute a topical allusion to an event in the recent memory of the book's readers (See Wilson 90). Adapted to my schema, Point A is the Babylonian captivity in the Sixth Century B.C.E. during which the book is set; Point B is the erection of a statue of Zeus in the Holy of Holies by Antiochus Epiphanes in 168 B.C.E.; and

Point C is 165 B.C.E. which represents the book's estimated date of composition. Nowhere does the Book of Daniel make its allusion to Antiochus specific. Rather, it is depicted in the manner of apocalyptic literature as described by Tripolitis: "in a cosmic setting, perceived not only as a local or national situation but one of universal significance." That is, it is given to us as an eschatological or "end time" event. (See, e.g., Dan. 8:17, 11:40, 12:9.) The reasons for this manner of writing are at least three, but the third reason is not sufficiently appreciated: (1) As stated, it creates "universal significance;" (2) It is safer for the author who is criticizing someone presently in power; and (3) Despite (2), the "hidden," topical meaning is clear to the intended (victimized) audience.

Now, the mistake that Wilson makes is that, faced with exactly the same narrative structure and a similar set of three identifiable points of reference in the synoptic gospels, he declines to make the obvious topical connection on the grounds that the allusion is *not specific enough*. He writes that "there is no concrete and inescapable reference, in any of the New Testament books, to the destruction of Jerusalem," assuming that the apocalyptics of Jesus were intended to have reference to that event (Wilson 253-56). Indeed, there is no concrete and inescapable reference in the Book of Daniel to Antiochus Epiphanes either, because apocalyptic literature does not work by means of such references, but rather by means of knowledge that is certain to be foremost in the minds of its readers and not in need of spelling out — a principle Wilson implicitly accepts as applied to the Book of Daniel, but rejects as applied the gospels. If Jesus meant to refer to the Roman destruction of Jerusalem, Wilson argues, why would he exhort his followers to head for the hills (Matt. 24:16, Mk. 13:14, Lk. 21:21) when Josephus tells us that at the time of the siege, the hills were full of Roman troops? (252-53). The answer is that, in apocalyptic literature, the references are not meant to be that specific. "Head for the hills" has the same meaning as "no one on the roof should go downstairs; no one should enter the house to retrieve anything; and no one in the field should turn back to get a coat" (Mk. 13:15-16 ASV; see also Matt. 15:17-18). These are not directions about where to stand on one's property, but figures meaning that the jig is up and the end of the world is at hand. But the end of the world has a very real meaning to Jews living in Point C: it has a meaning that is utterly inescapable and mentally oppressive. This is the historical fact that scholars have failed to imagine properly, even though the evidence for it amply exists; with respect to the gospel's eschatological predictions, the evidence is in Josephus. With respect to the form-functional parallel between (at least) the synoptic gospels and the Book of Daniel, it is in the imagery of the earlier and later books and in the explicit reference to the earlier book in the later books. Thus, not only the Son of Man and the abomination, but "not by human hands" (Dan. 2:34, 8:25, Mk. 14:58-59); "sleepers" awaking (Dan.12:2, Matt. 27:52); shining white or dazzling appearances [as also in Exodus] (Dan.12:10, Mk. 9:2-3, Matt. 17:2, 28:3-4, Lk. 9:29, 24:4, Jn. 20:12), the entire Man of Sorrows trope, etc. It's the same kind of book in the same kind of historical situation.

In fairness to Wilson, his argument against topical allusion to the destruction of Jerusalem is made in response to a claim made by J. Enoch Powell, which itself is too limited in its scope, and may be what throws Wilson off.[20] Nevertheless, in arguing that Luke's reference at 21:20, to "when you see Jerusalem encircled by armies" might just as easily be a topical reference to the approach to Jerusalem of a deputy of Caligula circa 40 C.E. as to the events of 70 C.E., Wilson is failing to appreciate the relative significance of the two historical events in the minds of Jewish and "Christian" readers at Point C: Caligula died and his deputy backed down (as Wilson himself notes), whereas 70 C.E. represented the demolition of the Jews' universe. And where, exactly, was Point C? Of course, scholars disagree about the exact dating of the gospels, but there is a fairly broad consensus for the composition of the gospel of Mark at about 70 C.E. If that dating is correct or even close — and if, as some credible scholars believe, all three synoptics were complete by 80 to 100 C.E.— how could anyone possibly imagine that the apocalyptic imagery of the gospels, in the minds of its first readers, *does* refer to Caligula's deputy, and that it does *not* refer to the destruction of Jerusalem?

It may be that someone in the field of religious studies, or perhaps some historian, presently believes that the destruction of Jerusalem was the catalytic event for the composition of Mark's gospel and the subsequent synoptics, but if so it is certainly not a widely-held belief. In my view, this fact results from the stranglehold that doctrine has on our historical imaginations and from the inability to appreciate the interrelationship of literary form and documented history, a type of book in a particular time.

To sum up, writers and scholars have already recognized: (1) a degree of allusion to the events of 70 C.E. in the apocalyptic imagery of the gospels; (2) evidence of midrashic composition of the gospels which eliminates literalist readings; (3) the contemporaneity of the destruction of Jerusalem in 70 C.E. and the composition of the first (Mark's) gospel; (4) historical confirmation of the tendency toward messianism as a response to Roman oppression, again, primarily through Josephus (See II:258-63); (5) recognition that the gospels are within the tradition of apocalyptic, prophetic literature as typified by Isaiah and Daniel. To this sum, I have added merely: (6) textually external, historical confirmation of messianism as a pattern of response to threatened cultural extinction, as seen in the Lakota; and (7) consideration of the relationship of the apocalyptic genre pattern to the most likely perceptions of world events in the minds of the gospels' contemporary readers.

Chapter 2

Matthew

The Matthean gospel is concerned in large part with a theme of competing legitimacy among Jewish sects. It thus begins with the pedigree of its protagonist, as a descendant of Jewish patriarch Abraham, and the greatest Jewish king, David. Some type of mystical numerology casts its sense of legitimacy as well, for we are informed that there were fourteen generations from Abraham to David, fourteen from David to the Babylonian Exile, and fourteen from the Babylonian Exile to "the Anointed" (Greek christos), that is, Jesus (1:1-17).

The fact that the pedigree is traced through Joseph suggests either that Joseph actually fathered Jesus out of wedlock without admitting it, or that the pedigree is claimed through the legal recognition of Joseph as the father, despite his not having fathered the child. The latter interpretation is consistent with the gospel's emphasis on the spiritual significance of things over the physical realities, because Joseph's acceptance of the illegitimate son legitimates Joseph as a good man, as much as it legitimates Jesus as the legal "son" of David. The true King of the Jews is thus not he who is born of Jewish kings, but he who is, is chosen by God.

In any event, we learn in the first chapter that Mary was "pregnant by the holy spirit," connoting illegitimacy. But through spiritual messages — a messenger of God who instructs Joseph in his dreams — the illegitimacy is legitimized, and Jesus is given the name that derives from Hebrew "Joshua," meaning "Yahweh is salvation." We learn that the name Jesus (Greek form of Hebrew Jeshua or Yeshua) means, "he will save his people from their sins." The titular term "Christ" or "Anointed" refers to being the chosen of God (a Jewish tradition); therefore the name

Jesus the Anointed, or Jesus Christ, has a meaning something like, "the God-appointed Savior" (1:18-25).

Our protagonist, therefore, has an allegorical name, because it matches his role exactly. The name is actually given to him by a messenger from God. A common fictional assumption one might make upon facts such as these is that one is reading a type of allegory. This assumption appears to be confirmed by the intro-duction of a second major theme in the first chapter, the fulfillment of prophecies. The prediction from the Hebrew Bible being fulfilled in the chapter on the birth of Jesus is said to be that "a virgin will conceive." It has been pointed out elsewhere that this tradition appears to have derived from a mistranslation in the Septuagint, or Greek translation of Hebrew texts, thought to have been used by the author of Matthew.[1] In today's NEB translation, the phrase from Isaiah 7:14 reads: "Therefore the Lord himself shall give you a sign: A young woman is with child, and she will bear a son, and will call him Immanuel." (Italics added). It is also true that the Greco-Roman world had knowledge of many virgin-birth religious traditions with which the Matthean author might possibly have felt obliged to compete. These include traditions associated with the births of Attis, Adonis, Aion, and Dionysus.[2] Whatever the inspiration for the detail, the virgin birth of Jesus is clearly presented to the reader as a fulfillment of prophecy, and not merely a miracle.

The fulfillment of this particular prophecy takes us back to that earlier question of who the father of Jesus actually was,[3] but since we are invited to perceive the birth and the sense of legitimacy in allegorical terms, we need not assume any physical father at all. This is a tale of the gods, in which virgins conceive. The legitimacy through David is not actual, but spiritual. Our hero is not an ordinary human being, but a divinely anointed savior of his people, fulfilling the prophecy of a Messiah.

Distinctions have been made between various levels of divinity attributable to Jesus. It is one thing to be a prophet, another to be a "son of God," another to be an all-powerful god oneself. The Jesus of the synoptic gospels, Mark, Matthew, and Luke, has been characterized as distinct from the Hellenistic deity of the gospel of John, who, as the Word (logos) of God, descends from heaven to be born and re-ascends after death.[4] The synoptic Jesus is less a timelessly existent, all-powerful emanation, and more of a man with powers of wisdom and magic conferred upon him by God, which does not make him all that different from other great men of the Greco-Roman world, such as deified Roman emperors. At this point, we need only recognize that the tale we are reading appears, in its early stages, to be an allegory about a divinely-appointed Jewish human being.

In Chapter 2, we learn that astrologers have seen a star which they understand to belong, somehow, to the "king of the Judeans." (The ASV uses "Judeans" instead of "Jews.") They follow the star to where it stops above the child. Aware of the star and the reports, King Herod is visibly shaken, a fact we can fully appreciate through the extra-textual historical fact, available through Josephus, that Herod is by designation the King of the Jews, or, in other words, Roman governor of Judaea. The astrologers avoid Herod by means of advice received in dreams, and they bring their gifts to the house containing the child. (There is no inn or manger in Matthew.) (2:1-12). The gifts of gold, frankincense, and myrrh are the same items that adorn the altar to Yahweh created by Moses in chapters 30 and 31 of Exodus. The reader is referred to Chapter 9, on midrash, for a brief discussion of the significance of the fact that the gospels are fashioned out of the materials of the Old Testament. The sources referred to in that chapter are available to those who wish a complete accounting of all the various close correspondences and loose parallels.

The dream messengers continue to protect Jesus by advising Joseph to flee with the child to Egypt, and then advising him when to return, once Herod dies (2:13-15).[5] They advise him also to settle in Galilee or Nazareth. The highly patterned narrative advances the two themes of legitimacy and fulfillment of prophecies, the first by creating parallels between Jesus and Moses, and the second by echoing passages from Hebrew texts. Thus, Matt. 2:17-18 refers to Jeremiah 31:15, and Matt. 2:22-23 alludes to Judges 13:5.

The development of character here is limited, since Jesus does nothing, yet it is significant insofar as the aura of power is created by the intervention of protective messengers (i.e., angels of God) who act to protect the infant Jesus, and by the parallels with Hebraic Scriptures, which are now cast as fulfilled prophecies in order to legitimize Jesus as the Jewish Messiah. Jesus is a magic being, with his own star, his own worshipers (the astrologers), his own band of angels, and the weight of Mosaic tradition aligned behind him. While yet a child, his powers overcome that of the great King Herod. This aura of divine authority and protection sets the stage for his entry into the story as a participant in the action.

The theme of legitimacy takes on the quality of something relative in the third chapter as John the Baptist, fulfilling prophecies of Isaiah, is clearly given a position of inferiority to Jesus, but superiority to the Pharisees and Sadducees, whom he calls "spawn of Satan." (3:7. The NEB's phrase is "viper's brood.") Since John is the predecessor of Jesus, he baptizes the younger prophet in the Jordan River at Jesus' direction, for the sake of form. The chapter ends with God's spirit descending in the form of a dove and with God's verbal approval of his "favored son," a complete slap at the Pharisees (3:13-17).

The conflict with the Pharisees and Sadducees is of course central to the story and part of the struggle for power in the Jewish community. From Josephus, we learn that the Pharisees and Sadducees were two of three Jewish schools of thought in the period we now refer to as the first century, the third being the

Essenes.[6] The Pharisees were the leading sect, and had effectively ruled Judea under a predecessor of Herod.[7] They were authorities in Jewish Law, believed in Fate, the imperishability of the soul, and its reward or punishment in an afterlife, whereas the Sadducees denied Fate, the soul's permanence, and its rewards or punishments.[8]

The strong antagonism toward the powerful Pharisees is here expressed as a false claim to legitimacy, in contrast to God's dove alighting on Jesus. The Pharisees, as John indicates, claim privilege through their claim of ancestry from Abraham. John growls that "God can raise up children for Abraham right out of these rocks" (3:9). Their illegitimacy derives from their lack of "change of heart" (3:8), initiating the theme of inner truth versus formal law, or truth versus the hypocrisy of the Pharisees. As we also remember from the first chapter, it is in fact Jesus, through Joseph, who legitimately traces his ancestry back to Abraham.

The apprenticeship or education or testing of Jesus occurs in the fourth chapter, as we learn that he is led into the wilderness by the spirit. The period of forty days and nights has a strong traditionary pedigree, which one can see reflected in Acts 1:3, and which apparently derives from the forty days and nights of deluge which Noah withstood in the ark (Gen. 7:4), or the forty days and nights Moses fasted alone in the presence of the God in Exodus 34:27-35. (Matt. 24:37 makes an explicit comparison between Noah's trial and the parousia.) In the wilderness, Jesus resists the three temptations of hunger, suicide, and lust for power. By refusing to make demands of God, he demonstrates submission to God, which then produces the magical protection of the heavenly messengers who attend him (4:1-11). This scene thus prefigures the lesson Jesus later teaches regarding self-sacrifice, that he who "loses" his life saves it and vice versa (10:39; 16:25).

Jesus next begins his career as a spiritual teacher in Capernaum-by-the-sea. The images seem archetypal, perhaps because these are the stories from which we have incorporated into our language such phrases as "seeing the light" and receiving one's "calling." As James and John come when Jesus calls, and as Jesus catches the fishermen, Peter and Andrew, he also travels about teaching in synagogues and practicing faith healing, so that his fame spreads (4:12-25).

The theme of Chapter 4 is thus the growth of power of the young magician-hero as he confirms his magical bona fides, assembles a following, performs and begins to grow famous. On an allegorical level, he represents the young man coming of age and realizing his capabilities as a productive member of society for the first time. Others are willing to accept him and benefit from his services, but he has first had to solidify his own identity by a process of adhering to his first principles. Had he not done so, Satan would have defeated him, and he would have had nothing to offer others.

The sermon delivered on the mountain, and which is famous as the Beatitudes, is a reformulation of Jewish law, delivered by a Jew to a Jewish audience, as Jesus makes clear by referring to "our ancestors" (5:21). The prophecy that not a serif will disappear from Jewish Law before that law and Jewish prophecies are fulfilled, after which the world disappears (5:18), would have been understood by the readers of a story written after the destruction of Jerusalem in 70 C.E., and set some forty years before the destruction took place. The message Jesus conveys in his first great speech is that the coming end of the Jewish world has meaning; that persecution leads to compensation "in heaven," meaning in the growth of the spirit, and that this growth is to be understood in a deepening of the commandments given to Moses: i.e., in a law that is both stricter in that it locates sin in its origins in thought (attitude toward oneself, 5:22, 29-30), and more generous and forgiving (attitude toward others, 5:39, 44).

The new idea in the Beatitudes is that sin begins not with an act, but with an evil thought. Killing begins with anger; adultery begins with lust. The rule is that one must govern oneself from the inside out, in contrast to the formalistic "scholars and Pharisees," who are portrayed as overly concerned with externals. At the end of Chapter 5, however, the focus is on nonviolence, generosity, love of one's enemies. A god of nature illustrates the point: God sends sun and rain indiscriminately. To take a similarly disinterested approach to one's fellow man would be an improvement over the state of Jewish Law that is no different than the actions of pagans: that is, identifying one's friends by tribalism and self-interest (5:45-48).

The attack on the hypocrisy of the formalistic Pharisees continues in the sixth chapter, which is devoted primarily to a condemnation of "grandstanding" in the practice of one's religious discipline. The Father is referred to as "the hidden one," with "his eye for the hidden" (6:6). Such language brings to mind a doctrinal approach favoring esoteric wisdom, an idea one encounters in various non-canonical "secret teachings" gospels, i.e., in gnosticism. On the other hand, gnosticism is not necessarily implied. This passage also relates to the idea previously delivered in the Beatitudes, that the heart is the source of goodness or evil. Obviously, if sin begins with a thought, God would have an "eye for the hidden," the secret thought or wish of the heart, and not just for the overt act.

From the end of the sixth chapter on, the character of Jesus is fully established, and his activities fall into a pattern. His character is that of magician, faith-healer, and legitimate authority as against the illegitimate "scholars and Pharisees." He is the true anointed Son of God, the true "Son of Adam" or true Jew, and the teacher of esoteric "inner" wisdom, or the doctrine of what I have termed "inside out," as opposed to formalist teachers of external law. He is a social and religious rebel (see 7:24-29), and a mover of public passions both good and ill. His pattern of behavior is to wander to and fro among the towns, villages, and other sites, preaching, healing, mystifying his followers, and constantly outwitting the Pharisees who increasingly fear and hate him and seek to entrap him.

When one reads looking for themes, they jump out of the text. The strongest of them is, as has already been mentioned, the theme of legitimate authority, which is of course the nominal meaning conveyed in the idea of being designated "the Anointed," but is also consistently given dramatic rendering in the conflicts with and diatribes against the Pharisees. In nearly every chapter, Jesus is either in direct conflict with the Pharisees, or is implicitly criticizing them, or is being implicitly preferred to them, as occurs in Chapter 17 where Moses and Elijah appear in conversation with him on a mountain, and the voice speaks from a cloud, saying, "This is my favored son," etc. (17:5). To be a favored son is something quite different than being an "only begotten" one. It implies other, less preferred sons. The contrast to the Sadducees and Pharisees is obviously intended, as they have just been attacked as hypocrites and sign-demanding formalists in the previous two chapters.

Interestingly, some of the more esoteric-seeming passages of chapters 15 and 16— those dealing with Jesus' mission to the "lost sheep of Israel" (15:24) and the reference to some here who "won't taste death" before the Son of Adam's imperial rule arrives (16:28) are easily understood in terms of the anachronistic structure of the book mentioned earlier. That is, if the imperial rule arrives when Second Temple Judaism ends, with the destruction of the temple in 70 C.E., then Israel's lost sheep would be saved at the same time the imperial rule arrives, namely, when Christianity "replaces" the old form of Judaism, in 70 C.E. At that time, there would be people still living who could remember back forty years or so to the time their teacher "predicted" this event, just as he routinely predicts his own demise at the hands of the false (and doomed) old guard.

This theme of legitimate authority is re-confirmed and most

strongly stated in Chapters 23 and 24. There, Jesus blatantly tells his followers not to be guided by the scholars and Pharisees, and not to use their terms of reverence ("Father," "Rabbi"). He damns them, says the blood of the innocent prophets is on their heads, and again uses imagery that is unquestionably intended to call up thoughts of the destruction of the temple. "Your house is being abandoned as a ruin ... not one stone will be left on top of another ... " and thus begins "the final agonies" (23:38, 24:2, 8). One of the methods by which Jesus establishes his credibility as founder of a new sect, therefore, is by means of accurately prophesying the destruction of the temple. The form of validation is external: the readers know about it from historical events which occur after the time period described in the story. The other predictions of Jesus — most notably that of his own demise (which is made analogous to the destruction of the temple, see, e.g., 12:57-62) are validated internally, through later events in the story itself. The other main method by which Jesus establishes his power is by means of magical acts or miracle-working. This power is sometimes portrayed as unsettling or frightful (8:34; 9:7), sometimes as cause for a party (two loaves and fishes banquets, 14:13-21, 15:32-38), and in at least one instance it is an act of mere vengeful spite: 21:18-22, in which a hungry Jesus causes a fig tree to wilt because it failed to offer him any figs.

When closely read as a work of fiction — meaning as a narrative text with self-defining epistemes, as opposed to a body of esoteric writing intended to be the basis for externally-imposed doctrines and beliefs — the theme of legitimate spiritual authority is much more powerful and consistent than the theme of resurrection. The resurrection theme is inconsistently handled in the book, and of somewhat less allegorical importance when contrasted with the legitimacy theme.

Resurrection as Allegory

It is clear from simply reading the text that the idea of resurrection from the dead does not begin with the resurrection of Jesus at the end of the story. It is one of Jesus' magical acts, performed at 9:18-26 (Jesus raises the dead daughter of an official, nameless in this version; a spontaneous wonder occurring both at and after the death of Jesus: with an earthquake the tombs open and "bodies of sleeping saints came back to life," etc., 27:51-53); a belief in the mind of Herod Antipas, 14:1-2; an apparent allegory, 10:39; 16:21-26 (the "lost life, found life" preachings); and by far most importantly, a disputed Jewish doctrine allegorically explained by Jesus himself (22:23-33).

We are told, in Chapter 22:23, that the Sadducees "maintain there is no resurrection." Josephus confirms that the Sadducees deny the soul's permanence, its punishment in Hades and especially "rewards".[9] Whether the doctrine of the resurrection is the same as that of the soul's permanence and its rewards or its punishments in Hades, it is clear that a doctrine involving something of this nature is a controversy among the Jewish sects in our fictional tale, and in Matthew Chapter 22, it is specifically addressed by our protagonist.

The context is an apparent trap the Sadducees set for him. It actually better fits the description of entrapment by means of a riddle, than the previous passage's trick question by the Pharisees, regarding the permissibility of paying the poll tax to the Roman emperor (22:15-23) which actually does receive that description. The Sadducees cite a law of Moses to the effect that the brother of a childless widower must marry the widow and produce offspring "for his brother." (22:24). They offer the scenario in which seven brothers marry the same woman, each brother dying in succession until finally the last one dies, followed by the widow's death, all without producing children. Whose wife is this multiple widow in the resurrection? they ask. Jesus tells them they "underestimate" the Scriptures and God's power, saying that at the resurrection people resemble heaven's messengers — not marrying — and then somewhat enigmatically he quotes Exodus 3:6, the word of God: "'I am the God of Abraham and the God of Isaac and the God of Jacob.' This is not the God of the dead," says Jesus, "only of the living." (22:32).

To dispose of the question of the resurrection by saying that the God of Abraham, Isaac, and Jacob is a God of the Living, is fairly obviously to speak allegorically, since Abraham, Isaac, and Jacob would seem to present the people of Israel, i.e., the Jews. An even more explicitly allegorical explanation occurs in the Luke gospel, where Jesus replies to the Sadducees: "That the dead are raised, Moses demonstrates in the passage about the bush: he calls the Lord 'the God of Abraham, the God of Isaac, and the God of Jacob.' So this is not the God of the dead, only of the living, since to him they are all alive.'" (Luke 20:37-38).

There is admittedly a degree of ambiguity in this story when one compares the separate accounts and different translations of it. For example, the referent in "to him" seems as if it could shift to God in the NEB translation of the Luke verse. But it is clear that Jesus finds in Exodus 3:6 the meaning of the concept of the resurrection of the dead. One then turns to Exodus 3:6 and finds God speaking to Moses from the burning bush, saying, "I am the god of your forefathers, the God of Abraham, etc." It does not really matter whether the aliveness of the forefathers exists in the mind of God or the mind of Moses — in fact, it is clearly both — because the point is that one's forefathers, although literally dead, are forever alive in one's mind. And that is the meaning of the resurrection explicitly espoused by Jesus.

This is a most interesting lesson for Jesus to give, because earlier in the Matthew gospel, Jesus has actually raised to life an apparently dead girl (9:18-26), and in the Luke narrative, at the same point in the story, he has already raised two dead children to life (Luke 7:11-17; 8:49-56). Presumably, if resurrection of the dead were to be given a literal meaning, it would not be given an allegorical one in this passage where Jesus himself is asked to explain it. It can hardly be assumed that the author of the narrative simply forgot the previous account(s) of children revived from apparent death, but rather it is more logical to assume that the earlier "resurrections" are to be understood allegorically: as hope given to the grief-stricken, as "good news" for those who need it. (The pattern is the same with the loaves and fishes miracles: they are alluded to with allegorical undertones in Matt. 16:11 et seq.)

These readings follow from the requirement of fictional consistency, meaning the harmonizing of premises previously given to us in the narrative itself. It is worth digressing for a moment, however, to point out that the allegorical reading is arguably even doctrinally consistent, when read with Christian documents composed before any gospel, namely the writings of Paul. In Romans, Chapters 5-7, Paul demonstrates his equation of death, sin, and the law on one hand, and life and the spirit on the other. He speaks of a potential acceptance of Christianity by his fellow Jews as "[n]othing less than life from the dead!" (Rom. 11:15); and in a long passage on life after death in the first letter to the Corinthians, he explains that once a seed is sown, "God clothes it with the body of his choice ... All flesh is not the same flesh: there is flesh of men, flesh of beasts, of birds, and of fishes — all different. There are heavenly bodies and earthly bodies ... " (1Cor. 15:38-40). The idea here, and further on in this extended passage, of the animal body planted as a seed followed by an implied harvest of a spiritual body, corresponds to the idea in Romans of spiritual growth away from a concept of God as tied to a "written code" (Rom. 7:6) and toward a concept of a spirituality accessible to Jew and Greek alike. (See Romans 3:29-31 and the frequent references to "Jew and Greek" in that book.) The Corinthians passage goes on: "What I mean, my brothers, is this: flesh and blood can never possess the kingdom of God ... the sting of death is sin, and sin gains its power from the law; but,

God be praised, he gives us the victory through our Lord Jesus Christ" (1Cor. 15:50; 56-57). In other words, death is the old Law, and resurrection is the new path leading to freedom from sin; Christianity thus accepts the law that "the wages of sin is death," but provides an antidote for this condition. To this extent, the doctrine of resurrection is not literal, although of course it is taken to be so elsewhere in Christian doctrinal writings.

To return to our narrative, after looking back at all the resurrection references in the story prior to the death of Jesus, one could also look forward to the resurrection of Jesus himself. In the story, Jesus has established his capacity for clairvoyance and prophecy, and he has already made remarks that appear to be predictions of his own eventual fate (17:12, 22-23; 20:17-19). In a passage that occurs after the Sadducee-resurrection argument, at 26:47-54, Jesus makes clear to his followers that he could call his Father's heavenly messengers to help him resist his arrest, but that he prefers to fulfill scriptural prophecies by allowing the "inevitable" things to occur. So the foreknowledge of his own resurrection is demonstrated prior to the Sadducee argument, and Jesus presumably knows all along of its purpose as fulfillment of prophecy. This resurrection, as well as the earlier one involving the official's daughter, is dramatically rendered as a literal rising from the dead. Unless we are to understand that both of these risings are spiritual in nature, however, i.e., the rising of "spiritual bodies" from the planting of a "seed" in the form of the human or "animal" body, then there is no reason for Jesus to explain the resurrection to the Sadducees as a consciousness of one's forefathers, rather than as a literal reality. He could have simply said that there are no marriages after the resurrection of the dead, and left it at that. Instead, he tells the Sadducees that the resurrected dead have bodies like God's messengers and that the resurrection means that God is a God of the living, because the consciousness of forefathers gives the forefathers a living quality in the mind of the living. To put it another way, the resurrection of the young girl, and even his own resurrection, must be like the allegory that Jesus describes to the Sadducees, because if they were not, the answer to the Sadducees would conform to the literal reality of these resurrections. If not, why not?

God's "messengers," it will be recalled, appear most often in dreams in the early chapters of the book, whereas at the very end they appear as a common vision to the stricken followers of the fallen leader. The dream has become a social vision, the common dream of a new religious sect. But we're getting ahead of ourselves a bit.

It remains to interpret, with fictional consistency, the last section of the Book of Matthew, devoted to the betrayal, torture, death, and resurrection of Jesus. In these passages, the allegorical premises come together in a fusion of intrinsic and extrinsic meanings that reveal a powerful symbol of the new Jewish vision. A key passage indicating the nature of this symbol is in 26:57-61, where Jesus is haled before the high priest Caiaphas to answer for alleged crimes. Two accusers claim that Jesus has boasted of being able to "destroy the temple of God and rebuild it within three days."

As the ASV notes point out, there is no passage in the Matthean gospel supporting the accusation.[10] However, there is the passage in Chapters 23-24, which has already been described, which apparently "predicts" the devastation of Jerusalem in 70 C.E. It is cast, in 24:15 et seq, as a future fulfillment of a prophecy of Daniel, which had reference originally to a desecration of the temple by a Syrian king in 167 C.E., as the notes again tell us.[11] Those notes continue: "In the style of apocalyptic literature,[12] the author of the gospel is referring to some recent event in the original readers' experience." And events from 68-70 C.E. are listed as possibilities.[13] The passage being explicated is one in which Jesus warns that "when you see the 'devastating desecration' ... standing 'in the holy place' (the reader had better figure out what this means), then the people in Judaea should head for the hills. ... " (24:15-16). Thus, the "fulfillment of prophecy" theme is accomplished by an inter-weaving of intrinsic and extrinsic meanings: allusions to Daniel and to events of 70 C.E., both seeming to predict things that have not yet occurred, are extrinsic; the references in Chapter 23 and 24 to desecration and destruction of the temple (23:38; 24:1-2) provide an intrinsic reference point for the Caiaphas passage in 26:57-62 — as does the subsequent mysterious tearing in two of the temple veil immediately following the death of Jesus, in 27:51.

The latter image, especially, demonstrates an allegorical parallel between temple and body, the body as the temple of the spirit. Thus, earlier references by Jesus to death followed by a raising after the third day (20:17-20; 17:22-23), conflated with a temple-body equation, could produce the accusation of the Caiaphas passage in 26:57-61. The accusers simply haven't understood what Jesus was talking about (i.e., his body, not the Jewish temple) — which is hardly unusual.

In the same episode, as rendered by Mark, at 14:57-59, the accusers say that Jesus claimed he would "destroy this temple made with hands and in three days I'll build another, not made with hands!" The testimony, however, is described as false, and we are told that "even then their stories did not agree." The reference to "not made with hands" apparently alludes to the Book of Daniel (see Dan. 2:34 and 8:25), in which the symbol of a stone or a power made "not by human hands" represents the power of God to destroy the idolatrous power of infidel kings. A temple "made with hands" can only be the Jerusalem temple. However, because of the "three days" reference which is supposed to refer to the period between Jesus' death and resurrection, the imagery is mixed and/or confused, which is essentially what the Mark gospel tells us. Later gospels will more strongly emphasize the temple-body equation.

If we follow up the (at least) implied equation of body/temple, the death of Jesus (or of any faithful man) is not merely the death of a man, but the destruction of a holy temple. If we then add to this idea the Daniel allusion, we have also a meaning related to the power of God or true religion to overcome temporal enemies. The destruction of the temple — a building "made with hands" — must be inevitably tied, in the minds of the story's contemporary readers, to that which took place in 70 C.E. during the Roman sack of Jerusalem. So the apocalyptic literature here is specifically prefiguring that tribal disaster because the images simply cannot fail to evoke it, and yet mixing into it the adumbration of resurrection, another form of God's triumph over the powers of this world.

The resurrection of Jesus as a common dream among his followers, represents a triumph which would not have been possible if the concept of the temple were limited solely to its literal meaning as a religious building located in Jerusalem. After the Jewish War, a way of life had ended for the Jews. A diaspora had occurred. The entire tendency of the gospels, and especially of the book of Matthew, is to blame the scholars, Pharisees, and Sadducees, for the corruption of religious law, even to imply that these Jewish factions are responsible for what will later happen to the Jews in the war. One sees this theme of accusation, for example, in the scene where Jesus himself feels forced to drive out the vendors from the temple (21:12-13); and we have the anti-Pharisaic diatribe of Chapter 23 ending with the image of Jerusalem's "house" as an abandoned ruin: "house" means both people and temple.

The allegorical and symbolic meaning of Jesus' death and resurrection is thus well-structured by means of intrinsic and extrinsic points of reference. A literal interpretation is amazingly poorly-structured, by contrast.

To begin with the death, there are the many images associated with it, and with events leading up to it, which carry out the strong and early-stated theme of fulfillment of prophecy. There is no need to catalogue them, as anyone with an annotated text can easily do so. Jesus' dying words, however, provide a perfect example of a detail utterly in keeping with the fulfilled-prophecy theme, while at the same time having no adequate intrinsic foundation whatsoever as something that it makes sense for Jesus to say. Those famous words — "My God, my God, why did you abandon me?" — from 27:46, "fulfill prophecy" by being a quotation from, and an echo of, the following passages from the Psalms:

My God, my God, why hast thou forsaken me and art so far from saving me, from heeding my groans?
—Psalms 22:1

I will say to God my rock, 'Why has thou forgotten me?'
Psalms 42:9

Thou, O god, art my refuge; why has thou rejected me?
Psalms 43:2

By means of these echoes, the verses of David are made to seem mere prefigurings of the passion of Jesus. In this way, too, the sense in which Jesus is the "Son of David" also becomes clear: he is his son in an allegorical sense, because David's words recur in the mouth of Jesus, where they are given new meaning. As usually happens with allegory, the original meaning is reduced in the process of allegorization, at least if one is reading the gospels doctrinally.

At the same time, a character who knew all along that his crucifixion was inevitable, and who refused to stop it from happening would have no reason to ask "why" God was failing him. To make this observation is to assume that the character, Jesus, is being portrayed here as feeling absolutely abandoned by

God. Given that this makes no sense as a thought in the mind of a supernatural being who has all along understood that this very fate is part of God's plan, we might reasonably question our assumption. Perhaps Jesus does not truly feel abandoned. Perhaps he is merely reciting Psalms which seem to him formally appropriate, the way he had John baptize him because it was formally appropriate to do so. These words of Jesus are often interpreted in just this way.[14]

The problem with such an interpretation is that it destroys the humanity of Jesus, and with it all sympathy for him as a character. If we assume that Jesus does not truly suffer, both physically and mentally, by spiritual anguish as well as physical agony, then the character is nothing but a puppeteer, using his own body for a controlled performance. In that case, there is nothing left of the story but an empty doctrine. By contrast, anyone who reads the story with sympathy for Jesus feels at this moment — "Why have you abandoned me?" — the focal point and high-water mark of tragedy. It is precisely at this moment that our man-god becomes truly human. Ironically, this is so because it is at this moment — and it is the one and only time in the whole story when this occurs — Jesus appears to have lost his faith. He feels forsaken by God as he dies.

Meanwhile, of course, the Matthean writer(s) surround this perfect moment of tragedy with pyrotechnics of magical portent: darkness at noon, the temple curtain mysteriously torn as if by an invisible hand, earthquake, tombs opening, dead saints coming to life and walking free, again echoing The Book of Daniel (27:45-54; Dan. 12:2). The story's flaw begins to crystallize, and it becomes more and more apparent as the tale proceeds to its close: the insistence on supernatural details disappoints. The story has already told the truth, and now it insists on covering the truth up. A tension arises between the actions of the Pharisees and the Roman guards on the one hand, and the followers of Jesus on the other. The villains seem rooted in the real world while the followers are caught up in a false-ringing and self-promulgated fantasy. This aesthetic disappointment of ours only materializes, however, if we have approached our story with a single empirical reality, being willing to make concessions to allegory, but not generally abandoning all sense of what is likely and what is unlikely when events are not supported by allegorical structure. The non-doctrinal reader finds the story's skeptics to be more convincing, not in terms of allegorical meaning, but in terms of what the "actual" events were.[15]

Look at what the Pharisees do. Afraid of a plot by Jesus' followers to steal the body and claim a resurrection, they secure the tomb with a stone and post a guard (27:62-66; See also Dan. 6:17). When an earthquake occurs, and the stone is rolled away and the body disappears, the guards spread the story that the disciples stole the body while they slept. The story circulates among the Jews "to this day" (28:1-15). We are told that the elders bribed the soldiers to spread the story, because the doctrinal position requires that the soldiers' story be demon- strated to be false. In fact, the story itself has provided us with characters who have a rational explanation for the empty tomb; it is this explanation that would be accepted as likely by anyone in today's world faced with a choice between this version of events and the one presented by the end of the story. Applying our single empirical reality, as fictionally modified by allegory, we reach this conclusion; whereas doctrine, and only doctrine, requires another interpretation. The book ends with the dream of the followers, and with the risen Jesus stating a pure doctrinal position: "All authority has been given to me." He urges profrom tizing (28:16-20).

As between the two groups, who are now perhaps identi- fiable in some embryonic sense as "Jews" and "Christians," it is the Jews who seem rooted in reality, albeit a rather corrupt one. Nothing about the meeting between the risen Jesus and his followers seems at all real or believable, except for one detail. It occurs in the last mention of any reaction or act of the followers, at 28:17: "And when they saw him, they paid him homage; but some were dubious." This dubiousness strikes the believable note, but it is not consistent with the followers as true believers.

The gospel of Matthew, then, as a fictional construction, leaves us with an unresolved tension between its allegorical meanings, its concessions to quasi-realistic character development (the passion of Jesus), and its unrealistic ending, which is made too literal-seeming to mesh well with the allegory. Artistically, it is a failure, and it must have seemed a doctrinal failure to the early Christians as well, because the gospel writers kept trying.

Chapter 3

Luke

... he has put the arrogant to rout. ... he has pulled the mighty down from their thrones, and exalted the lowly ... — Luke 1:51-52[1]

In Luke's gospel, the first public announcement of the birth of the Savior goes out, not to kings and potentates, as in Matthew, but to lowly shepherds (2:8-14). When Jesus is born in Bethlehem during the census-taking, he is placed in a feeding trough (2:7).

The characters with whom we are to sympathize are the lowly, the powerless, the poor but faithful ones. The disturbingly contrary predictions for the future of Jesus from God's messenger, Gabriel (that Mary's child will assume David's throne), and from Simeon, who says Jesus will be "a sign that is rejected" (1:32, 2:34), suggest that the spiritual destiny is exalted, but the earthly destiny is debased.

Luke's author says the story is a revision of earlier gospels (1:1-4), and two revisions in the Baptist-in-the-wilderness episode have significant effects. One is that the genealogy goes back beyond Abraham, all the way to Noah, Adam, and God (3:23-28). The other is that when the holy spirit descends on Jesus as a dove at his baptism, the voice from the sky does not merely approve of Jesus as a favored son, but rather it says, "You are my son; today I have become your father" (3:22). Taken together, these two revisions solve the problem of how Jesus can be a descendant of David without being the biological son of Joseph. In Luke, God's paternity of Jesus has its spiritual beginning at the moment of baptism, and its "biological" beginning at the creation of Adam. Whereas in Matthew, the pedigree through David was archly insisted on, in Luke, anyone could claim the same pedigree as Jesus simply by being baptized, since everyone is the child of Adam.

Preaching and healing in Luke represent forgiveness of sins, and more broadly, the opening up of God's grace to the gentile and the outcast. Thus, Jesus is seen and criticized for consorting with "sinners" (5:27-32; 7:36-50); for failing to observe priestly rules regarding eating, drinking, and teaching or performing work on the Sabbath (5:33-39; 6:1-11; 13:10-17; 14:1-6). His sermon on the plain ends with an exhortation not to judge others (6:36-49); and he performs faith-healing miracles for Romans as well as Jews (7:1-10).

As early as Chapter 4, Jesus has become a hated and feared figure, and an attempt is made on his life (4:28-30), because he preaches a message of inclusion that seems an affront to his own people. In his home town, he is not properly welcomed, and he tells two stories from Kings 1 and 2 in which prophecy and relief are afforded to non-Jews in apparent preference to the Israelites (4:24-27). As distinct from Matthew's gospel, which attacks the Pharisees from a point of view almost Essene-Jewish,[2] Luke's attack is on Jewishness itself as an exclusive club. Gone are Jesus' appeals to a common Jewish ancestry (see Matt. 5:21, 33).

In Chapter 8 Jesus re-defines the concept of family as "those who listen to God's message and do it" (8:19-21). These scenes are a refinement of the prophet-without-honor passage of Chapter 4, in which one's tribe is not defined by bloodlines or tradition, but by a quality of deserving established by other means, presumably faith.

In Matthew, Jesus offends the Pharisees, Sadducees, legal experts, and eventually the high priest. In Luke, he also offends against his home and his family. When, in Luke, Jesus does offend the Pharisees, he does it in a way consistent with his intemperate remarks about home and family: by a show of ingratitude. This occurs in Chapter 11, where he openly damns the Pharisees while sitting at a Pharisee's table. What the

Pharisees don't see is that, among his own followers, Jesus is much more self-controlled, and he extends this control over the followers almost tenderly, as if, indeed, they were his family (e.g., Chapter 12).

The radicalism of Jesus, on the other hand, can hardly be questioned. He rejects ordinary ideas of a home (9:58-62); of burial of the dead (9:60), of tribal loyalties (10:30-37), of Pharisaic hygiene (11:37-39), of adherence to creature comforts and the need to worry about such things as food and drink (12:15 et seq), of (as stated above) loyalty to family (14:25-27). He says:

> I came to set the earth on fire, and how I wish it were already ablaze! I have a baptism to be baptized with ... Do you suppose I came here to bring peace on earth? No, I tell you, on the contrary: conflict. As a result, from now on in any given house there will be five in conflict, three against two and two against three. Father will be pitted against son and son against father, mother against daughter and daughter against mother, mother-in-law against daughter-in-law and daughter-in-law against mother-in-law.
> — 12:49-53

It is difficult to believe that the original audience for this story (written ca. 80-100 C.E.)[3] could have read this image of dissension and factionalism without thinking of the war they had just undergone (ca. 66-70 C.E.). At great length, Josephus' history of the Jewish War describes the foolish and destructive dissensions among the Jews when the Romans, under Titus, attacked the city.[4] His words about the plight of women and children, about the envy of the dead, or about portentous earth-quakes,[5] remind one of Jesus' predictions of wars, insurrec-tions, and earthquakes in Luke 21, the sad plight of "pregnant women and nursing mothers in those days" (21:23), and his congratulations to the sterile in the times to come (23:28-30). The passage where Jesus longs to see the earth ablaze is of a piece with these predictions, not merely in tone, but because they seem to be connected by an allusion to Jesus' own upcoming passion.

The rest of the passage seems more closely tied to Chapter 21 by means of the imagery in both of fire, conflict, dissension, portentous weather, and so on. Chapter 21 makes no reference to a personal "baptism" nor does it otherwise seem clearly to allude to Jesus' own eventual crucifixion. Both passages describe scenes clearly evocative of the Jewish War: from the fire, conflict, and dissension of Chapter 12 to the even more explicit toppling of the stones of the temple (21:6), and the massing of armies at the gates of Jerusalem (21:20). The startling significance of the passage from Chapter 12, quoted above, is that Jesus seems to tie his own fate to the destruction of Jerusalem. After his speech, he says, in the ASV translation:

> *As a result,* from now on in any given house there will be five in conflict … [etc.] [Italics added]

If we can believe it, Jesus is saying that *his "baptism" is the cause* of the horrible and destructive dissensions that will afflict Jerusalem (or the "earth"). "Baptism" may mean crucifixion, but that crucifixion may symbolize the death of the Jewish capital, for crucifixion was the widely-inflicted Roman punishment for unruly Jews. The story of Jesus is a story of factional dissension among Jews. Dissension among Jews leads to the destruction of the Jewish homeland. The crucifixion of Jesus *as Jew,* at the insistence of Jewish priests, is the allegorical spearhead and catalytic event, and also a typical result of such dissension.

But look what follows the devastation, as Jesus describes it in Chapter 21:

> "… They will fall by the edge of the sword, and be taken-prisoner(and scattered) in all the foreign countries, and

Jerusalem will be overrun by pagans, until the period allotted to the pagans has run its course.

"And there will be portents in the sun and moon and stars, and on the earth nations will be dismayed in their confusion at the roar of the surging sea. People will faint from terror at the prospect of what is coming over the civilized world, for the heavenly forces will be shaken! *And then they will see the son of Adam coming on clouds with great power and splendor. ...* "

— 21:24-27

When read together, these two similar disaster predictions give us the suggestion of the martyrdom of Jesus superimposed on the destruction of Jerusalem and the Jewish diaspora of 70 C.E., or, in other words, we have the crucifixion of Jesus as an allegory of the Jewish nightmare, followed by the image of survival and resurgence of the spirit (the son of Adam coming on clouds, in the echo from Daniel 7:13). The "son of Adam" here represents both Jew and gentile, because the message of Jesus is consistently one of inclusion of the gentile and foreigner by a Jew (Jesus) with a more inclusive vision of true spirituality.

Seen as an allegory of the destruction of the Jewish world by the Romans in 70 C.E., the death of Jesus both explains the fate of the Jews and ties it to a universal concept of redemption. The insistent theme in these middle chapters of Luke, of the reversal of ordinary power structures, is also suggestive of a type of passive-resistive coping psychology which would be entirely consistent with members of an ethnic enclave under the oppressive domination of Rome. Such power reversals include the rhetorical power obtained through unstudied inspiration, to be used by persecuted Christians against more learned inquisitors (12:11-12); refusal to fear those with the power to kill (12:4-5); condemnation of the rich and exaltation of the poor (12:16-21 et seq; 14:13-24; Chapter 16; 18:23-25; 21:1-4); the reversal of the "first" and the "last" or the demotion of self-promoters (13:30; 14:11; 18:14; 17:33); the concern for the lost soul or sinner (Chapter 15; 18:9-14); and the idea of the hidden coming to light for those capable of right perception (12:2-3; 17:20-21 et seq). Jesus, as an emblem for an oppressed culture, embodies an almost total psychology of the oppressed, in which the powerless will have their day. That day, as has already been suggested, occurs simultaneously with utter self-immolation. Destruction becomes triumph.

Jesus compares his prophecy of necessary sufferings to the disasters in the time of Noah and Lot, both of which were apocalyptic. He ends with an exhortation to remember Lot's wife (17:31), saying:

> Whoever tries to hang on to life will forfeit it, but whoever forfeits life will preserve it. I tell you, on that night there will be two on one couch: one will be taken and the other left. There will be two women grinding together: one will be taken and the other left.
>
> — 17:33-36

His disciples ask, "Taken where, Lord?" and Jesus grimly replies: "Vultures collect wherever there's a carcass." (17:37).

In the *Jewish War*, as Josephus tells it, "the ground was nowhere visible through the corpses; but the soldiers had to clamber over heaps of bodies in pursuit of the fugitives."[6] Such circumstantial image parallels between the apocalyptic prophecies of Jesus and the war Josephus describes are too common to list, but more striking than any of them is the explanation Josephus gives for why the Jewish partisans went to war against first each other and then Rome, namely, "an ambiguous oracle, likewise found in their sacred scriptures, to the effect that at that time one from their country would become ruler of the world." A Roman collaborator, Josephus is quick to point out that the oracle referred to Vespasian, who came to power in Judaea, and that the carnage of the Jewish War of 70 C.E. revealed the folly of the Jews' interpretation of their messianic scripture.[7]

In Luke 17, Jesus says that *he is the cause of the troubles he predicts.* He came to set the world ablaze. Intra-family dissension occurs as a result of his "baptism" and his purpose to bring conflict, and it leads to "carcasses" in the streets. However, it is obvious that the crucifixion of Jesus did not literally precipitate the war, if only because it was reported to have occurred some thirty years before the events of 66-70 C.E. Thus, the connection Jesus makes to the known history of his audience is emblematic. *His story is that prophecy of a man from their country — a "King of the Jews" — who would rule the world* — but only by means of literary figuration. The story is an allegory. The speech Jesus gives in Chapter 17 makes that obvious. But it also reveals the allegorical meaning of resurrection, because of the time frame in which Jesus here alludes to it: the son of Adam is seen in glory in the clouds *after the catastrophe of the war.* Thus, the story of the teacher who is crucified at Golgotha on the Passover, and rises from the dead three days later is merely a microcosm of the macrocosmic meaning that a contemporary reader of Luke's gospel would necessarily understand: that of a resurrection of the spirit of a murdered culture.

This reading is consistent with the allegorical treatment of resurrection in the gospel of Luke. Resurrection occurs as an almost routine act of magic in two instances where Jesus raises two "dead" children; then it occurs when Jesus himself rises; but when Jesus explains the concept to the Pharisees, he explains it as the figurative idea that "resurrection" occurs in one's mind by virtue of the act of remembering one's dead. (20:27-39). This inconsistency makes little sense unless the entire story is an allegory of the refusal of a spiritual people to be destroyed. The raised dead in the story are tropes within the meaning of Jesus' allegorical explanation.

The failure, in 24:17-24, of Cleopas and Simon to recognize

the risen Jesus on the road to Emmaus makes no sense if the important point is that Jesus has actually risen from the dead. Why should the wonderful miracle not be immediately proclaimed? Why should the disciples imagine that they are talking to a total stranger, and a seriously uninformed one at that?

Consider *how* the truth comes out:

> … as soon as he took his place at table with them, he took a loaf, and gave a blessing, broke it, and started passing it out to them. *Then their eyes were opened and they recognized him … .*
> — 24:30-31 [italics added]

It is the bread of life, the spiritual meal, which has the same meaning here as the teaching that "wherever two or three are gathered together in my name, I will be there among them" (Matt. 18:20). Cleopas and Simon were hospitable to Jesus, the foreigner. They were "good Samaritans." They saw he was hungry and they gave him something to eat (Matt. 25:35; Is. 58:7). In short, when they follow the teachings of Jesus, based on love of one's neighbor and kindness to strangers, they "see" Jesus — and *not* before.

Once Cleopas and Simon "recognize" Jesus, it's a relatively easy task to inform the other followers that it was actually the Lord, raised from the dead, and that "they came to recognize him in the breaking of the bread" (24:35). Jesus then appears among the larger group, asks for food, and is given "a piece of grilled fish," completing the allusion back to the miracle of the loaves and fishes. (24:42). He explains scripture to them, and says that "all peoples" — notably not just Jews here — "will be called on to undergo a change of heart for the forgiveness of sins, beginning from Jerusalem" (24:47). And his last words, aside from an unspecified blessing, apparently allude to his prior predictions of the calamity to befall that city, which every contemporary reader of the book of Luke would have preeminently in mind. There would be a bittersweet note of the ominous in the last words of the Lord here, which is often missed by the modern reader:

> And be prepared: I am sending what my Father promised down on you. Stay here in the city until you are invested with power from on high.
> — 24:45-49.

That promise was to the daughters of Jerusalem that they would beg the mountains to fall on them (23:30), that "one will be taken and the other left" (17:36), that whoever tries to hang on to life will forfeit it, "but whoever forfeits life will preserve it" (17:33) – a promise in the form of a curse.

This image of one-taken-and-one-left recurs on the cross itself, where two thieves flank Jesus. One repents and the other does not. The one who repents (forfeits his past life) is accepted by Jesus into paradise (23:33-43). It also occurs in the ransom of Barabbas for Jesus by the people. Barabbas is a lost soul, and his life is saved. But Jesus forfeits his life, while saving his soul. (23:18-25).

To forfeit one's life is to give up one's past, to repent of one's sins, to receive a new life. When Jesus spoke of the destruction of Jerusalem in one breath, and in the next predicted the arrival of the son of Adam in the clouds as the denouement of the tragedy, he was making the actual destruction of the city of Jerusalem a figure for the forfeiting of one's past life, a life of sin, and offering in exchange for it a new life, based on charity, forgiveness, love, and kindness to strangers (because the Jews all became "strangers" at the diaspora). This is the allegory of the destruction of Jerusalem. Jerusalem's destruction is not only the thing alluded to, but also the thing which alludes. It is both fact and symbol, the middle allusion between the allegorical events in the life of the Anointed, and the meaning of spiritual rebirth for all mankind.

Chapter 4

John

At times, it seems as if one searches in vain for a readily-understood and reasonably brief translation of the Greek word Logos. The more one searches, the more one finds it necessary to pile qualification on qualification. Just for a sampling, here is the second-century Christian theologian Irenaeus of Lyon on the subject:

> In Greek, Logos as the directive faculty which elaborates thought is one thing, and another is the organ by means of which 'word' is emitted. Sometimes man remains motionless and silent, sometimes he speaks and acts ... ... But since God is all mind, all Word, all operative Spirit. ... processes and distinctions of this kind do not exist in him. ... God being all Mind and all Logos. ... his Reasoning is Logos and Logos is Mind and all-containing Mind is the Father himself. ... But when you scrutinize his [the Word's] generation from the Father and transfer the expression of the human word made with the tongue, to the Word of God, you yourselves rightly reveal that you know neither human nor divine matters.[1]

The foregoing, somewhat abbreviated passage from Irenaeus' attack on Gnostic heresies gives us a distinction inapplicable to God, a principle of unity (God is Mind, Logos, Father), and a warning not to equate human and divine concepts. The human word is not the divine Word (Logos), and human logos is not the same as the human word, inasmuch as the former may be unspoken, or is a faculty rather than a mere organ.

Antonía Tripolitis writes that the Stoics considered the Logos the supreme cosmic power, "a fiery substance" equated with divine reason or God. "the Logos is the organizing, integrating, and energizing principle of the whole universe."[2] Although Philo's later concept is "imprecise and often inconsistent," it is perhaps the one most resembling the idea in the gospel of John, since it is an intermediary being between transcendent God and matter, or "the first-begotten son of the uncreated Father."[3]

Logos is, in the phrase of Jacques Derrida, "God's infinite understanding." But the epoch of the logos contains "the difference between signified and signifier" which has now become "suspect."[4] All of Western metaphysics posits a being signified by a word, and an understanding of being, presence, difference, epistemology, based on this positing, but in fact God is no more than the word. How close this sounds to saying that the word "was what God was," but how different in implication!

Thus, in perplexity, we suggest the difficulties of interpreting the famous prologue of the Gospel of John, which begins:

> In the beginning there was the divine word and wisdom [Logos].
> The divine word and wisdom was there with God, and it was what God was. — (1:1)

Since Chapter 1 of this gospel revisits the account of creation, it is appropriate to note that *logos* is the significant emendation. It was something not specified in the Genesis account. It thus seems important, and yet we have no translation for it other than "the Word" (King James version) or "the divine word and wisdom" (ASV). Irenaeus confirms what the passage from John quoted above states: that the Logos is God. Logos is God's Reasoning, the elaborated all-encompassing Mind, the origin of everything, and the playing-out as well. And so to introduce this theological concept into creation is to assert some such idea as that all of life has a meaning, in as much as it derives from the reasoning mind that is, itself, God. Thus, one might take this prologue to be a kind of statement of purpose, which will be nothing less than to make sense of life, since all of life is the elaboration of divine reason (Logos).

The amazing thing about this opening chapter is not its ambition so much as its brevity and its beauty. The elaboration of the concept of Logos, like the elaboration of the concept of the Christ in Christian and Gnostic exegesis involves one in so many disturbingly confusing and sometimes meaningless abstractions — including paired concepts, tetrads, Powers, Emanations, etc. — that if, in fact, the opening chapter of John is in some way based on such esoteric Hellenistic theology, one has to admire its narrative restraint.[5]

The same can be said of the succeeding passages, because according to the Gnosticism that Ireneaeus deplores, it is the Christ, as an emanation from the Father (or some aspect of him) that comes down to Jesus in the form of a dove at his baptism, and which leaves him when he is betrayed and crucified.[6] Thus, one Gnostic interpretation of the baptism of Jesus in Chapter 1 of John's gospel would be of a descending and ascending spirit or god who or which is only temporarily associated with Jesus. The language of the gospel appears not to require us to make Gnostic interpretations in anything like the same degree to which we found it plausible, in the Book of Luke, to associate Jesus' predictions of apocalypse with the destruction of Jerusalem in 70 C.E. Despite the frequent theologizing for which the gospel of John is known and distinguished from the other, so-called synoptic gospels, there is no tendency to esoteric abstraction, and the theology is, if anything, more simple and straightforward than in the synoptics. "Rabbi, you are God's son!" declares the disciple Nathanael (1:49). Such flat-out proclamations are common in John, much less so in the synoptics.

For that reason, it is ironic that, instead of a miraculous dove actually descending on Jesus accompanied by a voice from the clouds at the baptism scene, the Johannine account presents the image as the vision of John the Baptist. "I have seen the spirit coming down like a dove out of the sky, and it hovered over him," the Baptist declares. "I have seen this and I have certified: This is God's son." (1:32, 34). What in Matthew and Luke was a miraculous occurrence is here reduced to a form of ecstatic utterance or figure of speech. However, there is plenty of magic in John's gospel.

The first miracle occurs when Jesus turns six stone water-jars kept for purification rites into wine for a wedding feast in Cana. He does this seemingly sacrilegious act at the request of his mother (who is not given a name), but not, apparently, to please her. In fact he displays what will turn out to be a persistent peevishness when she mentions the wine shortage. "Woman, what is it with you and me? It's not my time yet." Ignoring this incoherent remark, the mother tells the servants to do whatever Jesus tells them (2:4-5). She has evidently experienced his magical capabilities before and is convinced that he'll come through for the guests, despite his surliness. He does so, but we are told with obvious pointedness that the miracle "displayed his majesty, and his disciples believed in him." (2:11).

Three precedents are set in this episode, which become the pattern of the narrative and characterization of Jesus in this gospel. The first is the apparently incoherent reference to "not my time yet." As the story proceeds, Jesus will make several references to "his time," and in most cases he refers to his persecution and crucifixion. The meaning of the phrase is ultimately revealed in 16:19-24, where Jesus compares his own upcoming surrender to his enemies with the process of childbirth:

A woman suffers pain when she gives birth because the time has come. When her child is born, in her joy she no longer remembers her labor because a human being has come into the world. And so you are now going to grieve. But I'll see you again, and then you'll rejoice. ... — 16:21-22

So the coming of Jesus' "time" has a theological meaning with reference to the birth of the church. But this fact does not explain why Jesus would imply that a request for a harmless deed of magic ought properly to coincide with the birth labor associated with the nascent church. The detail lacks full coherence; nevertheless, we may perhaps refer to the "time" references as the ripeness motif.

The second precedent is the combativeness of Jesus' character in this gospel. His rudeness to his mother here is by no means unique.[7] His willingness to be offensive costs him disciples in 6:66. With little or no provocation, he is always telling his audiences that he is hated (7:7), that they are bent on killing him and are murderers (7:19, 8:37, 40, 44), that they will die in their sin (8:21, 24); that they are "children of the devil" who "don't belong to God" (8:44, 47), that they are liars who don't know God (8:55), while contrasting himself explicitly on such points — hardly a tactful or subtle approach. But there is a reason for it, as the third precedent will make clear.

The third precedent is that Jesus, in the gospel of John, does what he does for one reason only: so that people will "believe" in him. From the wedding in Cana, the John gospel proceeds apace to the temple in Jerusalem where Jesus drives out the bankers and animal peddlers by physically attacking them with a rope used as a whip. When the Judeans demand a miracle to justify his action — which must mean to show that he has some divine authority which would give them a reason to suppose his act is anything other than a mere assault — he doesn't provide one, but replies instead, "Destroy this temple and I'll resurrect it in three days." (2:13-18). We are told in a flash-forward aside that the remark does, in fact, refer to the miracle of his bodily resurrection, and so the disciples "came to believe" when they remembered this remark — as if the resurrection itself weren't enough! (2:21).

The connection between the second and third precedents is

that the gospel of John is driven by its insistent theme of the need to believe in Jesus. Those who don't believe are bad-mouthed *because* they don't. All the miracles occur *so that* people will believe. Because belief is the most important message, it doesn't matter that Jesus acts in ways that strike his hearers as mad or offensive, because *we* know that he's right. The result, from a purely literary point of view, is that dogma swallows up narrative credibility. Anyone who acted toward people the way John's Jesus acts toward his Pharisee audiences (and his own mother) would get no sympathy from a reader who was not already convinced of the divinity of Jesus. Judged as a human being in a social setting, he *does* seem hostile, paranoid, approaching madness at times. But his divinity is pre-announced, and the guilt of the Judeans is presupposed. "Isn't this the one they are trying to kill?" ask the Jerusalemites in 7:25, at a point in the story where, by comparison with the other gospels, no decision has yet been made by anyone to try to have Jesus killed.

For these reasons, if we did not already know that John's gospel is the most recent of the four canonical gospels to be composed, we would make that assumption, because from the text one can glean a familiarity with Jesus' fate and divine character that seems to presuppose a prior tale. Placing it fourth in the Biblical order would also allow the reader to fill in gaps in Jesus' character with nobler moments from the earlier gospels, while the present gospel hammers home the doctrinal themes for anyone who might have somehow missed them before.

Images of certain necessaries of life — bread, water, and light — occur and recur in the next several chapters, along with the paired contrasts of death/life and sight/blindness, to advance the strong message that belief in God's Word (which is what Jesus is) leads to life, and disbelief or rejection of the Word or Jesus is death or self-condemnation. Jesus is the bread of life and he offers life-giving water (6:33-51; 7:37-38; 4:10-15). He's also the "light of the world," who gives sight to the blind (3:19-21; 8:12; 9:1-5, 24-41; 12:35-38, 46). The metaphor of blindness and sight is actually turned for us in Chapter 9, after the Pharisees ban from the synagogue a "sinner" who had been cured of blindness by Jesus. Jesus questions the man, who acknowledges his belief, and then Jesus says, "I came into this world to hand down this verdict: the blind are to see and those with sight are to be blind" (9:39). These images of bread, water, and light (or sight) are images of spiritual life, which, we are told with metronomic regularity, is achieved through belief. The emphasis on the message is so strong and the images of life and vision are so consistent and so obviously metaphoric that some of the edge is taken off Jesus' vainglorious-sounding (compared to the other gospels) self-proclamations. It's easier to accept the speech in which Jesus tells the Judeans "I'm the one [Moses] wrote about" (5:39-47) if Jesus is an allegorical figure representing the Word of God.

On the other hand, even a purely literary reading devoid of the hermeneutical necessities of doctrine, cannot plausibly reduce John's Jesus to a pure figure of allegory. The weakness of allegory is its purity, its neatness. Jesus, as a character in John's gospel, and especially in the middle chapters, is ragged, patched together, sometimes an unbelievable cardboard cutout and sometimes more human, at times touchingly so.

Jack Miles (in *Christ*) has written convincingly about the sexual charge in the scene between Jesus and the Samaritan woman at Jacob's well, although the humanness of Jesus is here offset by the fact that Jesus is demonstrating his supernatural clairvoyance and also flatly claiming to be the Messiah (4:5-26). There is perhaps a frisson of flirtatious boasting that would harmonize the sexual tension with the power display, but it is too reductive to see as merely flirtatious Jesus' disregard of the taboo against fraternization between Samaritans and Judeans. When Jesus tells the woman that "God is not tied to any place," we are aware that this story all along has not been simply about a man, but about the will of God. A statement about God by Jesus carries significance and is a true statement about God's nature. The keynote of inclusiveness is struck, and it will reverberate in later chapters, as will the adumbration of the destruction of Jerusalem by the Romans, although it is not mentioned here.

One of the passages that has always struck me as revealing the humanity of Jesus is his rescue of the woman taken in adultery, which is often but not always located at 7:53-8:11. In the ubiquitous Johannine explanation, we are informed that the Pharisees and scholars intend to entrap Jesus by presenting him with the adulteress and the law of Moses requiring a stoning, but with typical intermittent obliquity, we are not told whether the trap would consist of her being stoned or not stoned. Evidently, the danger to Jesus is that whatever he answers will produce either a dead woman or the supposed violation of Mosaic Law.

The first element of this scene that seems peculiarly human, is Jesus' physical response of stooping and writing on the ground. It seems just the sort of evasive gesture that someone caught off guard would engage in, the sort of detail that someone would record because it happened, rather than because it had a meaning.

This naturally raises the question of what possible meaning the action might have. Miles sees in the sand drawing an image of "writing on the wall" reminiscent of scenes in the Book of Daniel, and also possibly Jesus' modesty in the face of the possibility that the woman's accusers might strip off her garments.[8] Philo of Alexandria, discussing the procedure for trying a woman accused of adultery, associates a lump of clay taken from the temple with a symbolic search for truth.[9] This might make for an effective symbolic reading if Jesus were writing on a lump of clay taken from the temple.

A simpler, although perhaps no more satisfactory effort to find meaning in the gesture of Jesus here is the contrast between writing on the ground and the commandments written on stone by the finger of Yahweh, one of which was "Thou shalt not commit adultery." Whatever the condition of the soil on which Jesus writes, the product is bound to be more ephemeral than stone tablets. Clearly, Jesus is revising the Law here. But what strikes one more forcibly than any symbolic meaning is the fact that Jesus seems to know he's in trouble, and that he has to think fast.

When he does it, this result, too, seems remarkably human. When no one throws the first rock because no one is sinless, Jesus says, "I don't condemn you either." One perfectly logical inference to be drawn is that he doesn't condemn her because he, too, does not consider himself sinless.

One gathers that the doctrinal reading would be, "Neither do I, who am without sin, condemn you," instead of, "Neither am I sinless, so I don't condemn you either." But the sinful-Jesus reading would be consistent with the remark of Jesus in Luke 18:19 and Matthew 19:17 to the effect that only God is good and/or that he himself is not rightly to be called good, or to be asked what is good. In such scenes, Jesus seems human because he acknowledges imperfection. The problem, of course, is that the humble, imperfect Jesus more properly belongs to the Lukan gospel than to the gospel of John. Nevertheless, this scene of compassion evokes our sympathies and admiration for Jesus in a way that all his "I AM" sayings and his condemnation of the unbelieving Jews does not.

It is the humanity of the Jesus character that prevents him from becoming a figure of pure allegory. One has no real feeling for Everyman or for Bunyan's Pilgrim. But there are many scenes in the gospel of John where one's feeling for Jesus results from his confrontation with or involvement in human dilemmas. Aside from the ones already mentioned, the principal such scenes are those in which Jesus himself is threatened, or where he is comforting his disciples for their anguish at being about to lose him.

The scenes where Jesus faces a threat tend to evoke sympathy, especially at the end of the story where the seriousness of the threat and the injustice of the punishment strike us most forcefully. In the middle chapters, our reaction is rather one of greater understanding of Jesus' thinking and teaching as he tries (with a slight suggestion of reasonable human fear) to explain himself to his accusers. The accusers speak first:

> "… We're not stoning you for some wonderful work, but for blasphemy — you, a mere human being, make yourself out to be God."
>
> Jesus answered them, "Isn't it written in your Law: 'I said, You are gods'? The scripture can't be wrong: if God has called them gods — those who got the word of God — do you mean to say about the one the Father set apart and sent to earth, 'You're blaspheming,' just because I said, 'I am God's son'? If I don't do my father's works, don't believe me; if I do, even if you can't believe in me, believe in the works, so that you'll fully understand that the Father is in me and I am in the Father." Again they tried to arrest him, but he escaped.
> — 10:33-39.

This is a mixed message, but the tone is considerably more conciliatory than it had been when Jesus was calling the Judeans liars and children of the devil. One half of the message is that one should not take too seriously language describing someone as a "son of God." According to the scriptures, says Jesus, everyone who gets the word of God is not only a child of God, but *is* a god. So says God, according to Jesus! But one senses the desperation in this argument. The reference is to Psalm 82:

> God takes his stand in the court of heaven to deliver judgment among the gods themselves.

...

This is my sentence: Gods you may be, sons all of you of a high god, yet you shall die as men die ...

The sense of Psalm 82 is not what Jesus implies in his defense. Very well then, Jesus argues, if you don't believe in me, then at least judge me by my works. Where's the harm in them? But at the same time he advances these nervous arguments, he refers to himself as one "set apart" by the Father and one mutually inclusive of the Father in identity.

The incoherence, the sophistical reasoning from fear, is a quality one wouldn't find in Everyman, but one recognizes it as a human tendency. And the willingness to downplay a doctrinal superiority, although one half of a message coming from both sides of our protagonist's mouth, again looks more human than godlike. Then, very human-like, Jesus "escapes."

What we have in the gospel of John, then, is a hybrid character. He is two-fifths human being, teacher, doctrinal innovator, and therefore fugitive from the Pharisaic Law, and three-fifths Divine Oracle, fountain of esoteric "I Am" sayings and overt claimant to the title of Messiah.

Ultimately, the success of the John gospel lies not in its characterization of Jesus, but in the way it ties its mechanical doctrines in with the story of the plot to kill Jesus. To understand this, we must first realize why the Judeans (fka Jews) want Jesus dead.

The first reference to systematic plotting to kill Jesus, as opposed to random fears and threats, comes in Chapter 11. Jesus has just raised Lazarus from the dead at Bethany. In keeping with the Johannine heavy doctrine, he does it with a public prayer of thanks to the Father, for the benefit of the onlookers, "so that they'll believe that you sent me" (11:42). The result of the miracle is that the onlookers divide into two camps: believers, and those who report to the Pharisees (11:45-46).

The priests and Pharisees call a council at which their fears about Jesus are given a definite political form:

> If we let him go on like this, everybody will come to believe in him. Then the Romans will come and destroy our <holy> place and our nation.
> — 11:48.

As Richard A. Horsley and John S. Hanson have pointed out, "the whole period of direct Roman rule [of Palestine] from 6 to 66 C.E. was marked by widespread discontent and periodic turbulence in Palestinian Jewish society."[10] "[O]ne of the concrete forms which social unrest took in the late second temple period was that of a group of followers gathered around a leader they had acclaimed as king."[11] Horsley and Hanson state that the conflict was "between the Jewish ruling group and the Romans on the one side and the Jewish peasantry on the other."[12] These conclusions about the state of Palestinian Jewish society in the time of Jesus are consistent with the story of the power relationships in John's gospel, in which a revolutionary, messianic movement largely among the peasantry creates a wolfish alliance between the ruling Jewish priestly class and the Roman governor.

The obvious fear of the Romans among the Pharisees' council members in the passage from John 11 quoted above is a fear which plays on another fear: the Roman fear of insurrection. The knowledge of this second fear is what leads to a plot to assassinate Jesus, as the chief priest Caiaphas argues:

> Don't you realize that it's to your advantage to have one person die for the people and not have the whole nation wiped out?
> — 11:50.

The idea is apparently that by allowing Jesus to continue his career while at the same time isolating him as an enemy of the state, Jesus can be made a scapegoat. This is exactly what happens, although Pontius Pilate is never fooled by the high priest into thinking that Jesus is actually a threat of the type he is made out to be, namely a "self-appointed king ... in rebellion against the emperor" (19:12).

Perhaps the most realistic character in the story, Pontius Pilate seems fascinated by Jesus. (The Soviet-era novelist Mikhail Bulgakov in his novel *The Master and Margarita* emphasizes and elaborates on this element of the gospel.) But he is successfully used by the Judean plotters, who managed to get the release of an actual rebel, Barabbas (18:40).

The notion of Caiaphas to have Jesus die to preserve the Jewish nation is expanded on by the narrator, but not, interestingly, into a universal concept of salvation. Rather, he states that Jesus would die "not only for the nation, but to gather together all God's dispersed children and make them one <people>" (11:52). The death of Jesus has this purpose of political and spiritual unification, not of metaphysical, sacrificial salvation.

Jesus himself comments on his purpose, in 10:17-18. "I am giving up my life so I can take it back again." This remark comes to us in a context that hearkens back to the earlier comment that "God is not tied to any place" (4:24). Jesus has been preaching in metaphors, referring to himself as both a shepherd and a pasture gate through which the sheep pass. (10:7-16). At the end of the speech he says, "Yet I have sheep from another fold, and I must lead them too. They'll recognize my voice, and there'll be one flock, one shepherd" (10:16). So Jesus is to give up his life as a Jew under the Law in order to take back his life as a more universal man. He gathers together (by his death) God's dispersed children and makes them one people, presumably meaning not only the dispersed Jews, but the Greeks also, after the fashion of Paul's preaching, which, as we know, preceded the composition of the gospel narratives. The famous hostility of

John's gospel to the Jews as a group ("Judeans" in the ASV) derives from the doctrine that "those who worship God must worship him as he truly is, without regard to place" (4:24), which means also, especially after the fall of Jerusalem in 70 C.E., without regard to ethnicity. When Jesus talks to the Jews he no longer speaks of "our ancestors," as he did in the gospel of Matthew, but rather he refers to "your law," as if it were not also his law, as a Jew himself.

So instead of saving the world through expiatory human sacrifice, the idea in John is unification of disparate groups through a death that is routinely referred to as a "glorification" (7:39; 12:16, 23, 28; 13:31-32). All these ideas come together in 12:20 et seq, when "some Greeks" come to Jerusalem to worship at Passover and ask to meet Jesus. Jesus is told of it:

> And Jesus responds: 'The time has come for the son of Adam to be glorified. I swear to God, unless the kernel of wheat falls to the earth and dies, it remains a single seed; but if it dies, it produces a great harvest.

To find one's life by losing it (the passage immediately following the one quoted above) here would mean giving up one's identity to take on a new one, i.e., forfeiting the Law for the new doctrine, which is the formula also of Pauline Christianity. As Jesus becomes famous among the gentiles, he recognizes his opportunity to plant a seed for the harvest. A voice from the sky confirms this sense of "glorification" and Jesus seems to connect this idea of a harvest of unity with the destruction of the Roman empire:

> "That voice did not come for me but for you," Jesus rejoined. "Now sentence is passed on this world; now the ruler of this world will be expelled."
> — 12:30-31.

He makes the same association between glorification and the condemnation of Rome in 16:11, as we shall see in a moment.

A stickler for formalist doctrines, the Johannine author gives us another reason why Jesus must die for this revolutionary system to play itself out. The first inkling of it occurs in Chapter 7. Jesus has been preaching about his "life-giving water," when the narrator takes us aside and says, "(He was talking about the spirit that those who believed in him were about to receive. You realize, of course, that there was no spirit as yet, since Jesus hadn't been glorified.)" (7:39).

No spirit yet? Glorification (betrayal and death) needed first?

Yes. Jesus explains how the spirit works in Chapters 14-16. The spirit goes by various names, depending on which translation or commentary one is using, and the names are: *advocate, paraclete, holy spirit,* and *spirit of truth.* The discussion of this spirit of truth comes in the context of Jesus commiserating with and comforting his followers over his impending death and the resulting separation there is to be between them. Anyone who has ever had a conversation with a loved one whom both conversants know to be dying can feel the emotion behind this particular doctrine, which, again, is a doctrine of unity.

Jesus leads up to this doctrine by first identifying himself with the Father, so that the disciples will have an image of God as a man (Son of Adam, Son of Man). They keep asking how to find their way to where he is going, and Jesus replies, "I am the way, and I am truth, and I am life" (14:6). They have seen the Father, because they have seen him (14:7). When he is gone, he will send the spirit of truth to them. The spirit will dwell in them and will unite them with the Father and with Jesus (14:15-21). They are to be glad that he goes to the Father "because the Father is greater than I am" (14:28).

For some reason, and perhaps it is only because he must reconcile them to his departure, he tells them that he can *only* send this uniting principle, the "advocate," to them if he goes to the Father (16:7). Jesus, being a vine through which God cultivates new wine (15:1-8), informs them that the advocate is the means by which they will instruct the world (16:8-15). Thus, we have a metaphor for the unity of humankind through the spirit of truth, a unity which overcomes death itself.

This spirit of truth which unites disparate peoples, even people separated by death, this spirit which plants a seed and harvests a new crop which is not limited in space or time, is the only formula for destroying the oppressor of the people: Rome, the great imperial power.

> ... When the advocate comes, it will convince the world of its error regarding sin, justification, and judgment: regarding sin because they don't believe in me; regarding justification because I am going to the Father and you won't see me anymore; regarding judgment *because the ruler of this world stands condemned.* ...
> — 16:8-11 [italics added]

The spirit of truth, to put it in a nutshell, will transform the world morally, doctrinally, and politically. It turns out that Jesus is, indeed, a king in rebellion against the emperor, that the kingdom of God opposes the Whore of Babylon. But the approach to revolution is holistic, inside out, moral and spiritual and *therefore* political, not an outside-only rebellion, such as Barabbas represents.

The classic works by S. Angus and Edward Gibbon (see Works Cited) about the transformation of the Greco-Roman world from paganism to Christianity — have emphasized that first Judaism and later Christianity appealed to people living in decadent times because of the emphasis these religions placed on ethics and/or because of the ethical devotion displayed by their adherents. So the birth of a new order whose "time had come" required not armies but ethical and spiritual transformation.

The method of transformation and revolution was nonvio-lence. The master and originator of the doctrine of turning the other cheek is he who tells Peter to "put the sword back in its scabbard" (18:11). For the true believers, it is an essential part of Jesus' form of nonviolence that it is pure renunciation, and not a tactic born of the necessity of utter powerlessness. In the same scene in which Jesus reprimands Peter for cutting off the ear of the slave Malchus, the very acknowledgment by Jesus that he is the one sought causes the Roman soldiers to fall to the ground (18:6). Jesus has the power at all times to resist, but he chooses not to.

This point is carefully maintained, as we are told that Jesus' penultimate words, "I'm thirsty" are spoken solely to fulfill scripture (19:28). Thus, the thirst is not real. And there is no poignant loss of faith, no truly human moment of despair or weakness at the end, as in other gospels, no cry at being forsaken by God. Except for a few passages where he is on the run, the Jesus of John's gospel begins and ends as a superman, the Hellenistic deity, as Burton Mack has observed, who descends to earth and ascends to heaven. [13]

The return of Jesus from the dead in John's gospel agrees not at all with the account in Luke. Mary of Magdala is the first to see him, and, supposing him to be a gardener, is startled into recog-nition by the sound of his voice. This story does not tally with the tale of Cleopas and Simon, awakened to recognition by the breaking of bread. Also, in this version, and for some unknown reason, Jesus cannot be touched until he has "gone back to the Father" (20:17). This detail makes no sense absent some esoteric doctrine of which we are unaware, considering that once he goes back to the Father he will presumably be untouchable because out of reach.

The resurrection appearances of Chapter 20 are, as we would expect from the Johannine author, utterly consistent in empha-sizing belief as the object of all the magic. The beloved disciple (who, according to tradition, is the John of Ephesus, said to be the author of this gospel, although the tradition is probably false) sees the empty tomb, "and he believed" (20:8). We can practically hear the fanfare. But the most famous object lesson is the way Jesus "showed them his hands and his side" (20:20). This is an absolute necessity for doubting Thomas the Twin, who refuses to believe without seeing the holes the nails made, and without putting his finger in the spear wound (20:25).

Magic works very selectively and purposely. It can cure medical conditions which have led to death. It can reverse death itself. But it doesn't close up wounds that are needed for identification by realists like Doubting Thomas.

The very last chapter gives us a reprise of perhaps the best-loved miracle of Jesus, that of the loaves and fishes. Jesus advises Peter and the others, while they are fishing unsuccessfully in the Sea of Tiberias, to cast their net on the right side of the boat, whereupon the empty net is suddenly bursting with schools of fish. In the ASV, they do not even have to bring their nets in, for:

> When they got to shore, they see a charcoal fire burning, with fish cooking on it, and some bread. Jesus says to them, *"Bring some of the fish you've just caught."*
> — 21:9-10 [italics added]

Do they want fish? Jesus has fish already cooking. Jesus produces fish in their nets. He was to teach them to be fishers for people. But the gospel of John adheres to literalism as well as metaphor, so these are real fish. Jesus *is* fish. The fish are magic, and so is bread.

Jesus says to them, "Come and eat."

None of the disciples dared ask, "Who are you?" They knew it was the Master. Jesus comes, takes the bread and gives it to them, and passes the fish around as well.

This was now the third time after he had been raised from

the dead that Jesus appeared to his disciples.
— 21:12-14.

Don't even ask why any of them would be thinking of asking him who he was if this is his third appearance. We don't ask this question, because it is a question that assumes normal realities of logic and recognition. We are not in the world of normal realities, but in the comforting, domestic environment of eternal and unceasing loaves and fishes. The image is pleasingly gustatory. We can almost smell the charcoal smoke. But the bread and the fish are not the nourishment of the body alone. They are the symbols of the human fish to be caught, and of the spiritual nourishment that one derives from absolute commitment to, and belief in, the Spirit of Truth.

Chapter 5

Mark

The first and leanest gospel is Mark's. That which is not contained in Mark could be considered embellishment, including much of the ending of this same gospel.

To begin with, the genealogy of Jesus, which we get in Matthew and Luke, is not found in Mark. Mark not only begins with the baptism scene, explicitly recognized as originating in Isaiah (40:3), but this gospel also has Jesus himself renouncing the idea that the Messiah must be a descendant of David. The Anointed, argues Jesus in 12:35-37, could not be David's son, when David refers to him as "my lord," a reference to Psalm 110. Thus, Mark's gospel makes no attempt to fulfill the prophecy that the Anointed prince will be descended from David, and there is no need to reconcile the fact that Jesus is not the biological son of David's descendant, Joseph, with the fact that a Messiah must be David's descendant. According to Mark's Jesus, the prophecy is incorrect.

Jesus has this tendency, which appears in the other gospels as well, of reading scripture outside the orthodoxies of his time. He is not a party man.

After the dove alights and the voice from heaven declares Jesus his favored son, the Spirit drives Jesus into the wilderness; that is, the desire for holiness, the God-desire or spiritual hunger of the neophyte holy man drives him to his religious solitude. The nature of the temptations of Satan during the forty days in the wilderness were embellishments in Matthew and Luke, insofar as the details are not given in Mark. For all we know, Mark's reference to Jesus being "put to the test by Satan" in 1:12-13, might refer to the fact that Jesus got hungry during a fast.

The initial healings are similar, and the connection between sin and physical infirmity is made clear by Jesus' question to the scholars: "Which is easier, to say to the paralytic, 'Your sins are forgiven,' or to say, 'Get up, pick up your mat and walk'?" (2:9). If this passage is read without a sense that the two acts, healing and forgiving, are somehow equivalent in meaning, then the question seems disjointed, as if Jesus were merely complaining that he had a right to do the easier of two tricks of the priestly trade. But if healing and forgiveness are doctrinal equivalents, then Jesus is simply saying that the scholars can't be angry with him for declining to do what is spiritually superfluous as well as physically difficult.

Physical laws resist; a miracle is a miracle because it is unlikely, incredible, impossible. In this regard, a comparative reading of the stopover in Bethany is revealing. In Mark, there is no story of Jesus raising his friend "Lazarus" from death. This "Lazarus" story appears only in the Gospel of John, but a version of its surrounding events occurs in each of the four gospels. We will call it the "Stopover in Bethany" because of its setting in Mark and Matthew. In each version, the details are curiously different, yet they seem to suggest symbols firing on the rough equivalency between forgiveness and healing.

For purposes of illustrating the argument, and because the details suggest this progression, I am going to assume that the first version of the story is Mark's, the second Matthew's, the third Luke's, and the last John's.[1] In the first version, then, which is Mark Chapter 14, it is two days before Passover and shortly before the betrayal of Jesus. Jesus stays in Bethany at the house of one "Simon the leper." An unidentified woman enters with an alabaster jar of myrrh. She breaks the jar and pours the myrrh on Jesus' head. We are told that "some were annoyed" at this extravagance (16:1-4). We are not told, specifically, who was annoyed. Jesus responds to the critics that there will be future opportunities to spend money on the poor, but it doesn't hurt to splurge a little now, because the woman is actually anointing him for his own burial (16:6-8). Judas Iscariot exits forthwith to cut his deal with the priests (14:10-11).

In Matthew, the time frame is the same. Jesus is in Bethany at the home of Simon the leper. Enter the woman with the alabaster jar of myrrh. She pours it over Jesus' head (Matt. 26:1-7). The story, in fact, is nearly exactly the same as in Mark, except that the critics of the woman's gesture are identified as "the disciples" (Matt. 26:8). This is a minor change, but it must be remembered that there are often many followers, hangers-on, and curious onlookers with Jesus' entourage wherever he goes. So, by referring to the disciples, the Matthew gospel specifically locates the source of dissatisfaction closer to Jesus himself; it's a kind of mini-mutiny among those who might be most sensitive to the appearance of hypocrisy or megalomania in their leader. Indeed, without some such reaction among Jesus' closest followers, the act of Judas Iscariot would lack motivation. It would simply be a mechanical fulfillment of prophecy.

Luke's story departs significantly from the outline. The Luke author, remember, has acknowledged using several previous sources in writing his story (Luke 1:1-4). The result is a fragmentation of the episode into several parts, and an attenuation of each part. The first part comes in Chapter 7, and occurs long before the Passover of the betrayal. Jesus has been travelling about, in Capernaum where he cures a deathly-ill slave (7:1-10), and in Nain where he revives a dead man and returns him to his mother (7:11-15). He is invited to dinner by a Pharisee named Simon. A local woman "who was a sinner" brings the alabaster jar, but instead of pouring it on Jesus' head, she anoints his feet after first weeping tears on and kissing his feet, and wiping the tears dry with her hair (Luke 7:36-38).

In this version of the story, it is the Pharisee, Simon, who thinks critical thoughts, not because of a waste of money that could be spent on the poor, but because the woman is a sinner. And because Jesus is not at the point of betrayal, death, or burial, his rejoinder to Simon is not about timeliness and the poor, but about Simon's own relative lack of devotion. "I walked into your house and you didn't offer me water for my feet. ... You didn't offer me a kiss ... You didn't anoint my head with oil," Jesus accuses Simon (Luke 7:44-46). He praises the woman's outpouring of love, and forgives her sins, with a little dig at Simon the Pharisee: " ... the one who is forgiven little shows little love" (Luke 7:47).

We can see from this first part of Luke's retelling that, insofar as the "stopover in Bethany" story is about a woman who seems to lavish improper attentions on the Master, it is no longer a story about the seeming-hubris of the Master nor about the proper beneficiaries of expensive generosity. Rather, it is about love and the forgiveness of sin. And what has happened to Simon the leper? He is now Simon the Pharisee. There is no loathsome disease, but Simon himself is the critic, not the disciples. The Pharisees are always the critics; they are, in fact, the enemies in all the gospels. The Pharisees are the moral lepers of these tales, but they are unforgiven because they are all law and no love. There is no cancer from within Jesus' own camp, but there is the moral condition which requires correction by means of forgiveness, or at least instruction in forgiveness of sins through love.

The other fragment of the story occurs in Luke Chapter 16, as part of the so-called "Travel Narrative" in which Jesus delivers parables and lessons to his followers as they make their way slowly to Jerusalem. It is not quite correct to refer to this passage as a "fragment" of the earlier story about the woman with the alabaster jar, but its images and names show it to be an intermediate link between that story and the later story of Lazarus in John's gospel. The passage is a parable, which must be quoted in its entirety in order to convey its full effect. The ASV version follows.

There was this rich man, who wore clothing fit for a king and who dined lavishly every day. This poor man, named Lazarus, languished at his gate, all covered with sores. He longed to eat what fell from the rich man's table. Dogs even used to come and lick his sores. It so happened that the poor man died and was carried by the heavenly messengers to be with Abraham. The rich man died too, and was buried.

From Hades, where he was being tortured, he looked up and saw Abraham a long way off and Lazarus with him. He called out, "Father Abraham, have pity on me! Send Lazarus to dip the tip of his finger in water and cool my tongue, for I am in torment in these flames."

But Abraham said, "My child, remember that you had good fortune in your lifetime, while Lazarus had it bad. Now he is being comforted here, and you are in torment. And besides all this, a great chasm has been set between us and you, so that even those who want to cross over from here to you cannot, and no one can cross over from that side to ours."

But he said, "Father, I beg you then, send him to my father's house — after all, I have five brothers — so he can warn them not to wind up in this place of torture."

But Abraham says, "They have Moses and the prophets; why don't they listen to them?"

"But they won't do that, father Abraham," he said.

"But, if someone appears to them from the dead, they'll have a change of heart."

<Abraham> said to him, "If they won't listen to Moses and the prophets, they won't be convinced even if someone were to rise from the dead."

— Luke 16:19-31.

We now have a character named Lazarus, who is a poor leper who receives comfort in the afterlife for his earthly sufferings, while a rich man is tormented in Hades, implicitly for having ignored people like Lazarus. (That's why it would make sense to warn the brothers.)

From this parable, the Oxford English Dictionary derives the words lazarus, "a poor and diseased person, usually one afflicted with a loathsome disease; esp. a leper," or an adjective to that effect; and lazarous, leprous. We also have the idea of raising Lazarus from the dead to effect a change of heart that will produce forgiveness for sin: the sin of the rich brothers who remain insensitive, and who ignore the law of Moses.

So now we have not only the common themes of forgiveness for sin, but a character who shares a condition with Simon the leper. A resurrection of Lazarus does not occur in Luke, and it is only a story Jesus tells. But the theme of the story is forgiveness of sin in both "pieces" of the "stopover in Bethany" (which is not Bethany in Luke).

We now have, in other words, all the figures used by John in his re-telling of the event in Chapters 11-12: a dead man named Lazarus, a resurrection, a woman who wipes Jesus' feet with expensive lotion, and an indignant reaction. In John Chapters 11 and 12, however, the author adds four unique details to these elements: (1) Lazarus is Jesus' friend; (2) his resurrection is actual; (3) the woman with the lotion is Mary, sister of Lazarus; and (4) the unfavorable reaction comes from Judas Iscariot! (John 11:1-44; 12:1-6).

Like Luke, John attenuates the Lazarus and foot-wiping episodes, but not nearly as much. Jesus first raises Lazarus at an undetermined time prior to the ultimate Passover, but in the very next chapter, he does the "stopover in Bethany," and it is six days before Passover (John 12:1). There is no hint of Mary's being a sinner. The objection Judas raises is the same one the disciples raised, but in John the motive is insincere. Thus, the interrogation by Judas:

"Why wasn't this lotion sold? It would bring a year's wages,

and the proceeds could have been given to the poor." (He didn't say this because he cared about the poor, but because he was a thief. He was in charge of the common purse and now and again would pilfer money put into it.)
— John 12:5-6.

The objection, in John, is pure villainy. There is no longer a seeming-legitimate concern with the appearance of prodigality, nor is there any connection between the anointing and a repentant act deserving of forgiveness. The object lesson approach to the idea of resurrection is abandoned: the inability to convince the rich to have a change of heart is no longer the point. And the lazarous leper is no longer a leper, but merely a dead friend raised for the sake of friendship and to convince the credulous masses to believe.

But doctrinally, if forgiveness of sin is equivalent to healing the infirm, then metaphorically the raising of a lazarus — or even the act of visiting a leper or a Pharisee — is equal to forgiving a lost soul. The problem is that John's gospel literalizes and oversimplifies both resurrection and objection, so that what we have is a dead man walking and a dastardly villain, instead of a misunderstood motive, a concept of forgiveness, or a caution to the worldly. John sacrifices the realistic nuance of Mark and Matthew, the ethical eloquence of Luke, and gives us instead doctrinaire melodrama. But if we look back through the prism of John's version through the other versions to the prototype, we can see that the meaning of Simon/Lazarus/Bethany/the woman is that true disease is of the soul, and that healing comes through forgiveness.

At the heart of this story, in all its four forms, is the idea of a human being rising from the dead. It is emphatically (except in John) not the idea of a god dying and rising from the dead. That idea was utterly common in both Greek religion and Near Eastern mystery religions of the Greco-Roman era. This distinction goes to the heart of the task of reading myth as fiction. Because Jesus, in the synoptic gospels at least, is a man — a charismatic Jewish wisdom teacher from a large family in Nazareth — and not a year-god like Attis, Osiris, Dionysus, or Mithra — his story is written as a human drama, not as a fantastic mythical enactment derived ultimately from the cycles of nature. The authors had imbibed those year-god myths and they echoed elements of them, but their narrations posited a human protagonist. For that reason, the stories read today more like fiction than could any Greek or Near Eastern myth. And when we read the four versions of the story as if they were fiction, we find the myth components breaking down, not matching up, not making consistent sense. The various authors could follow the human story more consistently than they could inject the year-daimon mythology into it.

One way to clarify this idea is to stay focused on the idea of resurrection in this first gospel. The world of the story is not so removed from our world in terms of the likelihood of such miracles. More specifically, the disciples of Jesus are described as uncomprehending when it comes to resurrections from the dead. Thus, after Jesus is seen by Peter, James, and John conversing with Moses and Elijah on a mountain, and after they hear a voice out of a cloud approving "my favored son," Jesus tells them not to tell what they have seen "until the son of Adam rise from the dead" (9:2-9). Their reaction:

> And they kept it to themselves, puzzling over what this could mean, this 'rising from the dead.'
> — 9:10

If we read this passage as fiction, we find an unexplained flaw in the construction. Why in the world are Peter, James, and John puzzling over what 'rising from the dead' could possibly mean, when in an earlier episode Jesus has raised a twelve-year old girl from death? (5:41-42). It was Peter, James, and John who were with Jesus when he raised Jairus' daughter (5:37). Don't they remember?

Details like this show that the story may not have been constructed with a plan from start to finish, the way a novel is, or that its plan had nothing to do with the consistency of fictional detail. More likely, it was cobbled together from many anecdotes, inventions, traditions, etc. Scholars have, of course, posited a hypothetical "Q Gospel," which consists of a collection of wisdom sayings from which both the gospels of Matthew and Luke drew. And virtually all of the Gnostic gospels are collections of sayings, rather than narrative-action tales, which helps us understand why the Jesus character seems to consist predominantly of a collection of wise sayings.

More to our purpose, however, we note that it is a myth component that breaks down in Chapter 9 when the very three insiders who were with Jesus when he raised Jairus' daughter are suddenly without a clue as to what Jesus can mean by "this 'rising from the dead.'" [2] Even more startling, Peter, James, and John have just at this moment seen and heard Jesus having a conversation with Moses and Elijah (9:2-6). Even if Jairus' daughter was only "sleeping," as Jesus said (5:39), one could hardly say the same for Moses and Elijah. And yet here are these three wondering, "What can it mean, this 'rising from the dead'?" It seems the characters of Peter, James, and John are unable to enter into the reality of their own story. They are outside it, bumping up against it with their faces to the glass, even though the miracles are transpiring right before their eyes. What accounts for this?

From a fictional perspective, one answer might be that Peter, James, and John inhabit the same empirical reality as does the reader. They represent the consciousness of the reader in the real world, unable to accept or understand the incredible miracles that unfold before him or her. We see miracles depicted, but we know that this kind of thing doesn't happen. The same is true of Peter, James, and John. [3]

In Mark, as in Matthew, Jesus performs not one, but two loaves-and-fishes miracles. (6:35-44; 8:1-9). After the first one, Jesus outdoes himself by walking on the sea and calming the winds. "By this time," the narrative reads, "[the disciples] were dumbfounded. (You see, they hadn't understood about the loaves; they were being obstinate.)" After the second demonstration, the disciples forget it as soon as it happens. Jesus loses patience with them and reminds them of both episodes:

" ... Don't you even remember how many baskets full of scraps you picked up when I broke up the five loaves for the five thousand?"

"Twelve," they reply to him.

"When I broke up the seven loaves for the four thousand, how many big baskets full of scraps did you pick up?"

And they say, "Seven."

And he repeats, "You still don't understand, do you?"

— 8:18-21.

But the quotidian mentality of the disciples goes beyond simple obstinacy and lack of comprehension of calendrical numerology. It approaches downright rebelliousness, an insistence on worldly common sense, especially in such matters as death and the possibility of rising from it:

He started teaching them that the son of Adam was destined to suffer a great deal, and be rejected by the elders and the ranking priests and the scholars, and be killed, and after three days rise. And he would say this openly. And Peter took him aside and began to lecture him. But he turned, noticed his disciples, and reprimanded Peter verbally:

"Get out of my sight, you Satan, you, because you're not

thinking in God's terms, but in human terms."
— 8:31-33.

This, then, is why the disciples are unable to interpret the events of the very story they inhabit: because they see things "in human terms."

This disjuncture between the "human terms" in which we, along with the dense disciples, tend to view things, and the mythical miracles which are "God's terms" is the characteristic that sets the gospels apart from most myths. It is a very awkward method of construction to have these human-thinking characters as the followers of Jesus, because it makes them seem incredibly stupid. They don't sufficiently inhabit their world, but rather they want to keep their feet in our own. But the point of constructing them this way is, of course, to tempt us to enter the mythical world through identification with these reluctant believers. It is a clumsy, unnecessary technique. The success of Christianity shows that people have always been willing to enter that mythical world, probably without identifying at all with those dunderheaded disciples.

In Chapter 4, we are told that Jesus spoke to his audiences in parables as a way of addressing "their ability to comprehend" (4:33). "Yet he would not say anything to them except by way of parable, but would spell everything out in private to his own disciples" (4:34). The apparent significance of this passage is that Jesus is content to let the crowds be mystified while allowing his circle of adherents to know the inner meanings. As is so often the case in reading the gospels, we are given the choice of reading this detail as the fulfillment of a prophecy (Isaiah 6:9: "You may listen and listen, but you will not understand.") or as a realistic detail, with human motivation and purpose. The two types of reading are mutually exclusive. If realistic, this passage has a curious effect, as if the disciples were too opaque to be able to decipher the meaning of a parable, whereas the more discerning listener would not need it spelled out. If "he would speak his message to them according to their ability to comprehend," it must mean that those who heard his parables could comprehend them. If not, what would be the point in delivering the parables?

This amounts to a problem or flaw in the logic of characterization. The disciples are intended (1) to be like us, and (2) to be special "insiders" second in importance only to the Master. However, (1) they are too stupid for us to consider them like ourselves; and (2) they seem at times less intelligent than the "outsiders," by virtue of needing special instructions in understanding parables. Certainly, when the narration has Jesus interrogating the disciples on how many baskets of scraps were left over after the loaves-and-fishes miracles, if we were to identify with the disciples rather than to laugh at them, we would feel as if we were being clubbed into submission on a very obvious point. This flaw results from the story's primitivism: the work is not written with a concept of fictional consistency, by which the characters would all have the same empirical or epistemological sense of the world they inhabit. Instead, because the work is a kind of tract for proselytizing, the realities are mixed, and the disciples, to the fiction-habituated mind, fall flat, believable neither as representations of real people nor as proper inhabitants of a fantasized world.

It is of course Jesus, and not the disciples, in whom we are mainly interested. The basis of our interest could be said to be artistic to the extent that it is not in an interested motive, not, that is, found in any overt search for doctrine or instruction that would benefit us. As opposed to the character who inhabits the Gnostic gospels as a mere name attached to cryptic sayings, the character in Mark and the other narrative versions manages to have both a personality and an enigmatic quality or lack of transparency characteristic of artistic forms of writing and characterization.

Chapter 7 can be used to demonstrate the facets of the

character. To summarize them in advance: Jesus is confrontational, provocative, principled, honest, tactless, apparently capable of ethnic derision but not fundamentally prejudiced. He is intellectual, secretive, and possessed of a sense of humor. Psychologically and dramatically, he is not a weak character, as the disciples are weak characters by virtue of being too easy to understand and too opaque to be credible.

The provocative, confrontational style of our main character is immediately apparent in the beginning of Chapter 7, as Jesus defends his disciples against the Pharisees' criticism that they don't wash before eating. Jesus sees in this criticism a formalism empty of devotion to God, and he likens it to the Pharisees' consecrating funds to God that they might have spent on their parents. In the latter case, the apparently devout instinct is really a betrayal of the commandment of Moses to honor one's parents (7:10-13). Jesus seems almost carping and adolescent in his insistence on opposing the Pharisees, but he says what he thinks, and his position derives from the principled belief, which is one of the main themes, if not the main theme of the story, that it is what is inside (the heart and mind) that counts.

The teaching of Mark 7:15 that "What goes into you can't defile you; what comes out of you can" is a corollary of Jesus' repeated axiom that the tree is judged by its fruit. Although the reference to "what comes out of you" is sometimes considered a scatological joke, the scatology does not refer to "what comes out." Rather, that which "comes out" refers to that which originates from within (the heart and mind), the various wicked intentions referred to in 7:22. The reference to the outhouse is simply to the place where those things that originate "from outside," i.e., comestibles, eventually end up (7:18-19). This principle of "inside out" characterizes Jesus more than any other; it is the quintessential Jesus.

We see what appears to be a type of ethnocentrism in Jesus when he refuses to cure the daughter of a Phoenician/Syrian woman of demon-possession, offering instead the rather cruel and dismissive remark, "Let the children be fed first, since it isn't good to take bread out of children's mouths and throw it to the dogs!" (7:27). The obliquity of this remark is astounding, unless it means what the facts of the scene seem to require it to mean: that the woman, because she is a Greek, is no better than a dog. But the ethnocentrism of Jesus is quickly overcome by something he sees in the woman that he apparently values: a quick wit. "Sir, even the dogs under the table get to eat scraps <dropped by> children!" she replies, and for that retort, Jesus cures the daughter (7:28-29 as worded in the ASV). We're reminded of the value Jesus places on good sense; "lack of good sense" ended the catalogue of evils he had earlier preached to his disciples (7:22). Good sense and a good sense of humor are required to allow oneself the pleasure of bestowing a benefit on someone who has bettered oneself in a bout of verbal sparring.

Throughout this chapter, based as it is on the idea that the heart is what counts, and not mere externals, Jesus has moved about and performed feats of healing without wanting his whereabouts and his magic to become known (7:24, 36). "But no matter how much he enjoined them, they spread it around all the more" (7:36). This desire for anonymity is both intriguing as a character trait and consistent with the theme of internal over external. Jesus is intellectually honest, concerned only with doing his work, and not with vulgar or self-serving display.

In this characterization of Jesus, then, we have an almost seamless weaving together of story theme and character trait, as well as certain peculiarities of expression or manner (the treatment of the Phoenician woman, the desire for secrecy) that give us pause, and force us to have to figure Jesus out. Jesus is a layered, complex, interesting character, unlike the disciples. The unity of development in a passage such as Chapter 7 makes us aware that whatever criticisms we may have of the treatment of the minor characters, the work as a whole is often a fine art.

In taking note of some of the sparer and/or different details of this gospel, particularly in the final scenes, we get a sense of what ends were achieved by later embellishment or retelling. In the Gethsemane betrayal, for example, "one of those standing around" slices off the ear of the high priest's slave (14:47). But in this version, the hothead is not named as Simon Peter, and Jesus does not magically re-attach the ear. What is lost is the development of Peter's unthinking, emotion-based devotion, as well as the disassociation of the followers of Jesus from any tendency to violence which has lasting effects. Only the Gospel of Mark gives us the detail of the young man who runs naked from his shroud as Jesus is deserted and seized (14:50-52). If this detail occurred in a modern fiction, it would immediately be seized upon as a symbol of death fleeing. In Chapter 15, the crucifixion scene, Jesus is flanked by other victims of the cruel punishment, but there is no good one who finds Jesus blameless and asks to be remembered, receiving thereby his commendation to paradise (15:29-32). Thus, there is no image of the idea that one is chosen and one left behind. Along with the fact that Jesus himself, in his final moments, does not forgive anyone for not knowing what they do, there is no embellishment of the notion of forgiving one's enemies or at least attaining to a final grace amidst persecution (See 15:33-37).

The most interesting ragged details come at the very end. One very minor one is that the associate of Mary of Magdala who accompanies her to the tomb site on two occasions is described in Chapter 15 as "Mary the mother of Joses" and in Chapter 16 as "Mary the mother of James and Salome." It is not important to decide whether Mary is, in fact, the mother of Joses, James, and Salome, or whether Magdala is accompanied by two different mothers named Mary on the two occasions, but the apparent raggedness of detail suggests a certain carelessness in composition, a certain patched-together tendency, which may after all be attributable to the nature of primitive writing materials, which made editing difficult.

The more important omission — if it can be called an omission — comes in the original ending. Here, as we have it in the ASV, Magdala and Mary the mother of James and Salome find the empty tomb and a young man in white who says Jesus was raised and will go ahead to Galilee, where they and the disciples will see him (16:4-7). They are to tell "Rock" (Peter) and the others, but they don't. Instead the story ends:

> And once they got outside, they ran away from the tomb, because great fear and excitement got the better of them. And they didn't breathe a word of it to anyone: talk about terrified …
>
> — 16:8

The ASV ends its Gospel of Mark there, providing the other, lengthier endings at the end of its collection. Its editors note:

> The scholarly consensus is that Mark originally ended with the abrupt stop at 16:8. The earliest Patristic evidence (Clement of Rome, Origen, Eusebius, and Jerome) gives no indication of any text beyond 16:8. In most manuscripts, however, Mark comes with endings which … are attempts to smooth out the abruptness of 16:8 and to harmonize Mark with the ending of the other gospels.
>
> — ASV 453-54

Obviously, the unedited, unembellished, or "unharmonized" version of Mark provides the greatest contrast between resurrection scenes, and so it is selected as the text for purposes of the contrast. It should not be surprising to the reader, then, to be confronted at the end of the story with the same problem encountered earlier involving the dramatic consistency of the unbelief of the followers of Jesus.

Lest "unbelief" sounds like too strong a word, I would ask the reader what a more appropriate word would be for the reaction of the women. They have been told by the young man in white that Jesus is "raised" and will meet them later, but instead of remembering Jesus' own acts of raising the dead, and finding the young man's suggestion to be plausible, they run away in terror. They are instructed by the young man to tell the other disciples, but instead "they didn't breathe a word of it to anyone" — a fact which, of course, can be true only in a fiction, unless the writer's facts come from someone (the young man in white?) other than the two women. If they told no one, no one would know, except an omniscient narrator.

What we have is the tension between the empirical reality known to the reader and previously imputed, unbelievably, to the disciples, and the dramatic logic, previously ignored, that would require the disciples and followers, such as Magdala and Mary the mother of Joses, to have some understanding that their Teacher was a magician who could defy any and all natural laws if and when he chose to. But the tension between those principles in this last scene does not lead us away from sympathy with the disciples, as it did when Peter, James, and John were puzzling over what "rising from the dead" could mean as the Master conferred with Moses and Elijah. Here, somehow, it is entirely believable that the women would be terrified, would say nothing of what they'd seen, and would run away. Why is this so?

In part, it is so because of the believability of the character of Jesus himself as a human being. When Jesus is meeting with Moses on the mountain, when voices speak out of clouds, when Jairus' daughter is raised from death, the reader posits a certain fictional convention. By means of a fictional convention, the reader accepts the miracles and assumes that the characters in the story should have to accept them as well — not as posing no diffi-culties to belief, but as having occurred despite their apparent impossibility. The disciples may be "obstinate" about the loaves and fishes, but they remember how many baskets of scraps were left. But the completed story has given us something else besides miracles. It has given us the complex Jesus character of Chapter 7, the pathos of the murder of a good man at the hands of authority acting at the behest of a passionate and unprincipled mob, the image of death faced bravely, but not without fear and suffering. It has given us an image of something acutely real, which could be abbreviated as our own fear of death.

For that reason, the final scene takes place in the real world, as it were. The disappeared body and the frightened women create a dramatic satisfaction which is greater than that achieved with the emended endings. By not making everything explicit, the original story opens up a question for the reader: was it true? Such a question is a dramatic convention for the reader, by means of which the philosophical questions arise. The body is gone, the women are terrified: end of story. To ask the reader to decide what is true at that point, or whether Jesus really rose or not, is to ask the reader to determine what values are important in the story he or she has just read. It is to ask what lives on, what can never die. In that way, a dramatic convention gives rise to philosophical questions.

Such an ending is preferable, in the fiction-habituated mind, to one in which Jesus' resurrection is spelled out, and in which we are told that the disciples carry the message throughout the world, or are recognized as authentic by their power to handle snakes, and so on. In fiction, once the premise is set up, a suggestion provokes more thought than a dissertation. In that proper balancing lies the art.

Chapter 6

Acts: The Fantastic History of the Apostles

A major premise of this book has been that we approach the fictional text with a fixed and single sense of empirical reality. There is no assumption that all readers necessarily believe the same kinds of things, but that most readers at least have a stable sense of what is believable in the "real world" and what is not, so that they are not changing their minds about it from one day to the next. However, it is assumed that there is a fairly broad consensus about the distinction between the natural and the supernatural event, so that even people whose belief system incorporates aspects of the supernatural are able to make the same assumptions about what a "supernatural" event is, e.g., one not conforming to ordinary and commonly-known laws of physics, biology, or other science. Walking on water, virgin birth, rising from the dead, and so on, would commonly be understood as supernatural events — a simple idea. For purposes of the fictional reading, then, we declined to adopt a second sense of empirical reality which allows us to accept such supernatural occurrences as facts in their "unique" time and place. That double sense, we argued, is the province and requirement of doctrine, not of fictional interpretation.[1]

In the process of reading the gospels, we discovered that some of the supernatural events in some of the texts could be read as having an allegorical, or even a symbolic meaning. Most notably, the image of resurrection from death is made more open-ended by means of its different treatment in various places where it occurs as a theme or an image in the texts. Similarly, we were able to see some symbolic significance in the miracle of the loaves and fishes. By contrast, certain other supernatural events lack symbolic resonance: walking on water, water turned to wine, causing the fig tree to wither, etc. Some of these events have a basis in Hellenistic or Egyptian myth, but in this book we have not addressed mythical archetypes. These events have no internally cognizable symbolism; therefore, for us, they appear as mere *literal* occurrences in the narrative.

As *literal* occurrences — events that are narrated solely because they "happened" in the story — their appeal to us, as readers making no doctrinal allowances, is limited to the appeal of fantasy. Lacking deeper meaning, the fantastic detail has greater or lesser appeal to the reader of fiction purely to the extent that he or she "likes that kind of thing," has a taste for it.

Pure fantasy, like history, like any form of narration limited in its interest to the surface detail, achieves its interest by means of storytelling, by which is meant the power, as E.M. Forster described it, "of making the audience want to know what happens next." [2] Whether the appeal of a piece of information lies in its supposed reliability as fact (the appeal of history) or in its escapism (the appeal of pure fantasy), that appeal lies in the information itself and not in a semiological layering. As Todorov has observed, "poetry cannot be fantastic."[3]

In our own day, we tend to see fantasy and history as being at opposite ends of the spectrum of appeal: the readers of the former are not likely also often to be readers of the latter. However, from the perspective of our fixed empirical reality, the Acts of the Apostles appears to be a combination of those two types of "surface level" writing. In fact, what we ought perhaps to realize is that this particular genre existed in the ancient and medieval world, but does not exist today: the fantastic history.

The fantastic history is something entirely different from the historical fantasy. We have the latter genre today, usually in the form of "alternate history" science fiction. (The premise of a popular fantasy novel some years ago might be stated, "What if the Nazis had won World War II?")[4] And some would include also the historical romance, although I would argue against applying the word *fantasy* solely to implausible plots. What we do not have today is the fantastic history: the factual account or record of a historical phenomenon of social interest — the history, in this case, of the birth of the Christian church — accompanied by propagandistic episodes in which the known laws of physics, biology, or otherwise of science or nature are defied. Here is an example of this type of writing from Bede's history of the English church, written in 731 C.E.:

> Saint Alban, who ardently desired a speedy martyrdom, approached the river, and as he raised his eyes to heaven in prayer, the river ran dry in its bed and left him a way to cross. ...
>
> As he reached the summit, holy Alban asked God to give him water, and at once a perennial spring bubbled up at his feet — a sign to all present that it was at the martyr's prayer that the river also had dried in its course. ... But the river, having performed its due service, gave proof of its obedience, and returned to its natural course. Here, then, the gallant martyr met his death, and received the crown of life which God has promised to those who love him. But the man whose impious hand struck off that pious head was not permitted to boast of his deed, for as the martyr's head fell, the executioner's eyes dropped out on the ground.[5]

While today we speak of "laws of physics" in a way that probably derives from the Age of Reason, we must not imagine that the medieval world of Bede, or even the ancient Greco-Roman world, had no such sense of how objects in nature typically behaved. It is clear that they did, and that the very impact of fantastic histories such as Bede's depended on the perception of the reader that such things as were being described were extraordinary. As Todorov has put it, "... the limit between matter and mind is not unknown [in fantastic literature], as it is in mythical thought. ... ;

it remains present, in order to furnish the pretext for incessant transgressions."[6] That limit-transgressing in a type of literature is made possible by the perception in the reader of the limit.

Obviously, the ancient mind had a sense of reality and unreality that was similar to our own, and it is not necessary to catalogue all the possible differences. However, one significant difference between the ancient and modern minds was that in the ancient and medieval worlds there existed a greater sense of awe in the face of the mysteries of nature, which expressed itself as a belief in deity. It has often been remarked that nature was fearsome to man in past times when he had to deal with it more directly than is necessary today. It has become axiomatic that magic and religion both arise as means of accommodating and placating the awesomeness of nature. Nature is only overcome by supernature. Perhaps the most ready example for our purposes is the religious concept of sacrifice as a method of placating the gods. The idea has of course attached itself to Christianity, despite a lack of clear derivation from the gospels. The pertinent point is that the apparent rules of nature could always be overcome in the mind of someone for whom nature itself loomed very large and fearsome. It is this sense of things that Hamlet communicates when he tells his rationalist friend, "There are more things in heaven and earth, Horatio, than are dreamt of in your philosophy." This is the sense of the vastness, the overwhelmingness of nature. Perhaps the better way to think of the idea here is to say that Nature was once big enough to *include* supernature. The opposite and more modern feeling is found in Freud, who wrote of the "oceanic" sensation of eternity described by those of a religious bent, and concluded: "I cannot discover this 'oceanic' feeling in myself."[7]

In that contrast of sensations lies the reason, in large measure, for the possibility of fantastic histories in the ancient world, and the impossibility of there being such a genre today. The Age of Reason has intervened. Since then, we have drawn a curtain of technology between ourselves and the awesome lonely vastness and power of nature. Today, the television is always on, with its flickering and vapid comfort, its endlessly chattering human voices, absolutely forbidding serious thoughts and non-commercial states of mind. Or else it's the internet connection, with its own forms of white noise. For us today, history is one thing, and the supernatural event is quite another: fantasy.

But in the Acts of the Apostles, as in Bede later, we get both history *and* fantasy. (We continue to get both for many centuries — until, for example, the time of Marco Polo.) The first half of the Acts, devoted to the apostle Peter, is the more heavily fantastic section by far. In it, Jesus ascends physically into the sky (1:9); Judas Iscariot drops dead on a plot of land he buys with his thirty pieces of silver, and his entrails burst out (1:18); Ananias (the first one) is upbraided by Peter for not participating fully in the apostles' communistic economic system, whereupon Ananias promptly drops dead (5:1-5); followed soon thereafter by his wife, under a similar curse from Peter (5:7-10). The sick are cured by Peter's shadow falling on them as he passes by in the streets of Jerusalem (5:15-16). Peter raises Tabitha from the dead (9:36-40). Angels and earthquakes repeatedly release the apostles from captivity (5:19, 12:6-7, 16:25-27). Paul strikes a sorcerer blind by invoking the Lord's power (13:11). Herod is stricken down by an angel for usurping the honor due to God, and, in a most curious narrative order, "he was eaten up with worms and died" (12:23).

The second half of the Acts of the Apostles is more dominated by the other type of writing to be found in the book, namely history, which is often also in the form of travelogue, as the first person plural narrator becomes increasingly present. "When it was decided that we should sail for Italy," he (Luke?) writes (27:1). "We ran under the lee of a small island called Cauda. ... " (27:11). "The fourteenth night came and we were still drifting in the Sea of Adria" (27:27). And so on. The historically interesting detail is unmistakable at times: "It was in Antioch that the disciples first got the name of Christians" (11:26).

What is noticeably lacking in the Acts, whether we are reading a fantastic legend or a factually plausible historic account, is any semiological or symbolic resonance, any invitation to reflect on levels of meaning, any trope, or even any ethical philosophy, such as the parables of Jesus tended to evoke. All the books of the New Testament are arguably propaganda, but the Acts of the Apostles, like much of the gospel of John, offers its propaganda transparently and coercively. If Ananias and his wife fall dead because they have withheld some of their money from the apostolic commune, it is not for us to wonder how it is that they came to be dead. We are to accept that they died mysteriously, supernaturally, and as a consequence of their lies to God, and any other suspicion is clearly heresy. There is less wiggle room here for allegory than there was when Jesus made his enigmatic statements about the stones of the temple at Jerusalem.

We are now faced with an issue that has been deflected, deferred, and downplayed as being not of major interest to us until now. It is that despite the clear differences among the various books we have discussed, it is fairly obvious that a common authorial intention can be imputed to these works which must sooner or later be factored in if we are to understand the genre distinctions we are making. That intention is clearly doctrinal. These works were written to give body, focus, and doctrinal substance to the young church that had sprung up around the figures of Peter, James, John, Paul, Barnabas, Silas, and the others. The mysterious Christology of Paul could not, by itself, have sustained the church; and it is clear that there were oral traditions already circulating: wisdom sayings, if nothing else. If, then, there was a common evangelical purpose, what accounts for the tonal, modal, and executional differences that allow us to say that one finished product is like an allegory, while another is like a tract, and a third is a rather two-dimensional fantastic history?

One answer might be *talent,* but since the large doctrinal purpose is the same in each case, and since the effects we see are not consistent within any one given work, we may assume that the literary accomplishment of Luke's gospel — and this is by far the best-written, the most literary gospel — is largely unconscious. The same can be said of the other synoptic gospels. Their authors are not intending necessarily to create poetry. Poetry is that high use of language in which meaning blossoms out in layered petals, expanding continually, deepening, then moving in many directions at once, a life-creating force. Propaganda, by contrast, is deadening: coercive, rigid, threatening. Believe or die: those are the only choices offered by propaganda in its strongest forms. Despite its mystically beautiful beginning and its lovely and poetic ending, the gospel of John is essentially a propaganda piece. The Acts of the Apostles is emphatically so. If the scholars did not tell us that Luke and Acts were written by the same person we might imagine that the author of Acts is merely puffing his work when he makes the connection. It wouldn't be the first time a sequel writer made the identification; sometimes such identification is purely convention — identifying narrators rather than authors — and it is curious that Luke's gospel does not describe anything like the forty-day sojourn of the resurrected Jesus among the apostles in Acts 1:3. One wonders if the writer of Acts means that Jesus appeared again after the departure or ascension,[8] but parts of the farewell speech (1:4-5) sound significantly similar to the one in Luke that it seems to describe the same moment.

If the gospel of Luke and the Acts of the Apostles were written by the same author, the greater literary quality of the former could derive from the fact that the materials used to create each work were significantly different. For the gospel narrative, Luke had the accounts of "original eyewitnesses and ministers of the word" and "many ... orderly narrative[s]" which were sufficient, in their sum, to require "thorough research" (Luke 1:1-3). By contrast, the Acts appears to be based on fewer sources and less traditiony ones. Much of the last half of it reads as if it were a journalistic, first-person memoir. Acts has been called an "adventure story;"[9] and such stories don't require the semiological intricacy of parables, allegories, and symbols.

But if the use of such tropes occurs in the synoptic gospels despite a doctrinal intention for which flat propaganda might have served as well, we can only go on speculating as to why it occurs. When gospel narratives were first felt to be needed, were "Mark," "Matthew," and later "Luke" first sought out because of their reputation as good storytellers? Did their ability as storytellers lead them, unconsciously, into forms and tropes inherent in that art which, by the very nature of such forms and tropes, produced results too nuanced and subtle for the purposes of propaganda? When these storytelling powers proved too literary to promote sound indoctrination, did "John" seek to correct the problem with his mind-numbing mantra, "and then they believed"? Is the book of the Acts, with its series of miracles and preachments, intended to "nail down" the adherents which the synoptic gospels might leave with too much doctrinal leeway?

These are questions for historical scholars. We can raise them because we notice the differences in form and style, but form and style do not provide the answers. We are not supposed to care about authorial intentions, and we don't, as a rule. But when art gives way to propaganda, the author makes his presence felt as an irritation, a kinesis of the inartistic, such as Joyce's Stephen Daedalus describes in *A Portrait of the Artist as a Young Man*.[10] When the stillness and purity of art fades and we feel ourselves being pushed, we are curious about who is doing the pushing and why.

This is not to say that the fantastic history, the travelogue, and adventure in the Acts do not make for a good read. But they do not have the same power as the gospels (even including John) to lead the reader into reflection. On its surface level, however, the Acts creates several interesting characters, instead of just the one in the gospels, and these provide a contrast in their method of characterization.

The most obvious contrast is that between Peter and Paul. Peter has a legendary heroic quality, while Paul seems more the apprentice mage. Paul strikes people blind (13:11), but Peter strikes them dead (5:5-10). Angels escort Peter out of prison (5:19-20), but Paul does well to survive a stoning (14:19-20). As already mentioned, the vast bulk of miracles are associated with Peter. The power of his very shadow to heal the sick, and the impunity with which he curses the first Ananias and his wife Sapphira to death for failing to contribute enough money to the Christian commune, make him practically a divine figure, for gods are never murder suspects. One is tempted to dust off one's copy of *Anatomy of Criticism* to nail the classification, and there one finds that gods inhabit myths while humans involved in adventures inhabit romances: both genres are mythopoeic, says the author of the *Anatomy*.[11] It is clear that Peter himself is not a god, and that his string of adventures constitutes the legendary romance which is sequel to the myth. Yet Paul seems to occupy a level beneath the legendary-heroic one on which Peter operates.

This point could provoke an argument, because Paul has legendary-heroic moments: he works "signs and miracles" (14:3), carries out Christ-like faith healing (14:8-10), foretells the future (27:22-24), and handles vipers without being harmed (28:3-6). Rather like Peter's shadow, Paul's scarves and handkerchiefs have the power to cure disease and demon possession (19:11-12). But alongside such wonder-working episodes, and seemingly in greater number, are all the passages in which, unlike Peter, Paul seems all too human. Such episodes create for Paul a kind of see-through realism, a layer of apparent historicity beneath the legend, so that the legend, applied to him, remains only a kind of mannerism.

When the citizens of Lystra, impressed by Paul's curing of a crippled man, declare Paul to be the god Mercury and his associate Barnabas to be Jupiter, the two apostles are horrified. And when the crowd attempts to offer them a sacrifice of oxen, they react by tearing their clothes, and rushing into the crowd shouting, "Men, what is this that you are doing? We are only human beings, no less mortal than you" (14:14-15). To be sure, the horror that Paul and Barnabas express here stems as much from their revulsion at pagan rites of animal sacrifice as at the notion that they should be worshipped as immortals, for they go on to excoriate the Lystrans for "these follies," and to indicate that the true nature of the living God is to be seen in the natural phenomena of rain, crops in season, food and good cheer (14:15-17). But there is no similar outright declaration of mortal humanity by Peter.

Even the manner of Paul's healing the cripple has a suspect quality, in the form of a psychological element:

At Lystra sat a crippled man, lame from birth, who had never walked in his life. This man listened while Paul was speaking. Paul fixed his eyes on him and saw that he had the faith to be cured, so he said to him in a loud voice, 'Stand up straight on your feet'; and he sprang up and started to walk.
— 14:8-10.

That fixing of the eyes and its resulting discernment of sufficient faith is an emphasis subtly different than those in the healings by Jesus, and certainly than the emphases in the cures done by Peter. The typical pattern for Jesus would be to effect the cure and then say to the restored person, "Your faith has cured you," or some such phrase. Here, the emphasis on Paul's seeing something in the man who sits listening to him almost suggests a tacit collaboration.

There is an earthy practicality to the controversies

surrounding Paul. While Peter is obsessed with his vision of the formerly unkosher animals on the sail cloth (10:10-16 passim) Paul finds that his own proselytizing efforts at Ephesus lead him into a conflict with a sort of primitive union or guild of silversmiths whose livelihood in creating statuettes of the goddess Diana is threatened by the new religion (19:23-41). The resolution of the uproar is much more mundane than the miraculous escapes from prison Peter achieves with the help of angels. In Paul's case, the town clerk simply dismisses the angry crowd of artisans for lack of sufficient evidence and improper legal process (19:37-41). The reader has also the ironic awareness that, in fact, Paul's preachings *do* amount to a form of sacrilege against the pagan gods, despite the town clerk's willingness to let him off.

This sense that Paul is somehow getting away with things — fooling the crowds by curing impostors or escaping charges of blasphemy against the pagan gods whose rites he openly considers "follies" — raises an issue that goes back once more to genre. The question is whether we should also read the Acts as fiction rather than as history. We have thus far argued that Acts is a melange of fantastic history (Peter and some of Paul) and plausible fact-based history (other parts of Paul's story). The question about fictionality develops from the sense that both Paul and Peter may well be getting away with things when the actions of each are viewed from a skeptical, rationalist or realist viewpoint. Specifically, viewed as we today would view history, at least three events have raised the following questions: (1) How did Ananias and Sapphira really die? (2) Was the crippled man actually an impostor or an audience plant seeking to help promote Paul's ministry? (3) Why is Paul considered by the town clerk at Ephesus to "have committed no sacrilege and uttered no blasphemy against our goddess" when in fact it was part of Paul's teaching that "gods made by human hands are not gods at all" as Demetrius the silversmith alleges? (*See* 19:37, 26). Fact-based history has an answer for the third question: as previously stated, there wasn't enough evidence, and legal process was insufficient. But most readers of the Acts would never bother to ask the first two questions, whereas if the book were written today, no rational historian would ignore them.

Obviously, the doctrinal reader ignores such questions because of doctrine: that double-mindedness which we have discussed in previous chapters, whereby acceptance on faith precludes all normal empirical analysis with respect to any story in the Bible. But there is another double-mindedness that is created when we admit the existence of the extinct genre of fantastic history. We read of the death of Ananias and Sapphira, and of Paul's cure of the crippled man; we peg it as legendary, and we read on. Another approach we might take is to read the Acts as fiction. The genre question that arises is, therefore, why one would choose to read the Acts as fantastic history rather than simply as fiction?

While some might consider that an answer to this question expresses no more than a personal preference, I believe that the preference is best made on the basis of an analysis of its relative capacity to yield useful information. By information, I don't mean simply data, and by "useful" I don't mean practical. Rather, the question should be, which epistemological stance enables us to learn the most about the phenomenon we are examining? In approaching the gospels as fiction, there was much to learn, in part because the previous investigations had used that avenue the least, and in part because the gospels are written in a manner that in many ways resembles fiction. The Acts are both less well investigated and less like fiction. The book contains at least one indisputably historical figure: Paul, whose own writing, according to the scholars, makes up a large part of the work attributed to him in the New Testament. There is also another factually and historically undisputed "character" in the Acts, which is the church. Because the historical basis for the Acts is more visible than in the gospels, and because the Acts makes much less use of figurative language or tropes than do the gospels, there is arguably more to be learned by studying this work as history than as fiction. I have chosen the term "fantastic history" rather than history, because many of its details are fantastic. The terms "legend" and "legendary history" should also be rejected as too dismissive of the knowledge of actual history that is gleanable from the Acts. By "fantastic history," I mean a history which contains fantastic elements, but otherwise has some basis in events that may be supposed to have occurred.

That said, it seems to me that we are not prevented from discovering a fiction-like tendency to characterize by means of form-dictated consistency, rather than by strict adherence to known facts, or, conversely, to find in known or alleged facts a pattern of characterization analogous to fictional characterization by form-dictated consistency. Such characterization can be seen in the contrast between the more realistic Paul and the more legendary Peter, because it is Paul who undergoes a transition from a villain to a hero. As Saul, he persecutes the Christians and approves the stoning-to-death of Stephen (7:59-60). Of all the characters in the Acts, only Paul undergoes what today would be called realistic development, meaning the step-by-step detailing of growth, change, alteration.

There is much more to Paul's conversion than simply the emblematic story repeatedly told about his seeing the light on the road to Damascus (9:3-9; 22:6-11; 26:12-18). Moreso than in history, significance in fiction derives from structure, and it may be no accident that of all the many characters in the Acts, three of them are developed by means of their own long speeches.[12] The three are Peter, Paul, and Stephen. Stephen's one long speech is doctrinally insignificant for Christians. It is a re-hashing of Jewish history, intended to demonstrate to the council of elders his Jewish bona fides. It is Stephen's defense against charges of blaspheming the Mosaic Law (6:11-15). Unfortunately, or perhaps perversely, it ends with an accusation of heathenism and guilt for the murder of Jesus, and with Stephen's deliberately provocative claim to see, through a "rift in the sky," the Son of Man standing at God's right hand (7:51-56). So Stephen is chased from Jerusalem and stoned outside its walls, where, we are told, "[t]he witnesses laid their coats at the feet of a young man named Saul" (7:57-59).

This is a pivotal moment in the narrative. Although Saul does not yet realize it, it is the beginning of his transformation into the apostle Paul. Stephen is a Jew who sees the rejection of Jesus as a flaw of Judaism; Paul is a Jew who rejects Jesus and approves the murder of one of his followers. Stephen wins the contest, overcoming death and giving new life to Saul, who is reborn as Paul. Understood this way, Paul's various statements about resurrection in his letters make a great deal of sense, *e.g.*: "… you must regard yourselves as dead to sin and alive to God, in union with Christ Jesus" (Rom. 6:11). These are the words of someone who must have begun to feel like a murderer until he changed sides and accepted forgiveness and a new identity.

Because Paul, unlike Peter, first appears as a murderous villain, or at least as a misguided persecutor, and then changes and develops, it is fictionally appropriate for him to be treated as a more realistic, less legendary figure. (At the same time there is something trope-like about Paul, in his re-born state, being cared for in his first three days of light-flash blindness by a man with the same name as the Ananias who was cursed to death by Peter. But we may take this as a coincidence, since Peter does not represent death for Christians!) I speak here only of an *analogy* to fictional development. There is also a historical reason why Paul looms less legendary and has more human believability than Peter, which is that the author of the Acts evidently traveled a great deal with Paul. Thus, the first half of the Acts reads like a set of stories or legends one has been told, whereas the last half, Paul's half, reads like a travelogue of first-hand observations. According to Eusebius, Luke wrote the Acts "not this time from hearsay [as he did the gospel] but from the evidence of his own eyes." He was alleged by Eusebius, however, not to have been the companion of Peter, but of Paul.[13]

Chapter 7

A Vague Apocalyptic?

In his highly readable book on the Apostle Paul, A.N. Wilson takes the time to dispute the likelihood of topical allusion in the gospels to the events of 70 C.E. Inasmuch as I have argued in favor of the topical allusion, I should like to address the issues raised in Wilson's book and clarify my own position on the issue as a whole. However, I want to begin by observing that for most critics and scholars of the New Testament, or those that I have read, the events of 70 C.E. do not receive anything like the attention they deserve, and it is to Wilson's credit that he even deals directly with the issue.

Wilson's argument is in response to the claim of J. Enoch Powell to the effect that the reference in the Matthew gospel to the "abomination of desolation" is a topical allusion to the Roman siege of Jerusalem. Wilson's first objection is that all three synoptic gospels have Jesus advising his hearers to "flee to the hills" upon seeing the abomination, whereas Josephus tells us that at the time of the siege, the hills were full of Roman troops.[1] The implication is that Jesus, if he were predicting the siege, would not be advising his followers to run into the arms of their enemies.

Wilson seems to believe that the strongest claim to the topical allusion is thought by its proponents to be Luke's reference, at 21:20, to "when you see Jerusalem encircled by armies." But he thinks that a topical reference might just as easily be to the approach to Jerusalem of a deputy of Caligula circa 40 C.E., and that Mark would have a better claim to a topical reference to 70 C.E. because he would know more about the siege details than would Luke. Wilson flirts with the idea of a pre-war composition date for the gospels of Mark and Matthew, but finally rejects it, and thinks it surprising that that "there is no concrete and inescapable reference, in any of the New Testament books, to the destruction of Jerusalem," assuming that the apocalyptics of Jesus were intended to have reference to that event.[2] "How convenient it would be for the historian," he writes, "if, instead of this 'let the reader understand,' Mark had written, 'let the reader understand that this is a reference to the tragic events of 70 in which our faithful brethren in the Jerusalem church were all put to the sword.' But no such specific reference exists" which will help date the gospels.[3]

This argument is riddled with perplexing inconsistencies and blind spots. The first area of perplexity arises with respect to the precision of reference. Recall that the original idea Wilson objects to is that the "abomination of desolation" in Matthew 24:15 is a prediction of the Roman destruction of Jerusalem. That is, he is focusing on Enoch Powell's claim, which limits the topical reference to the "abomination of desolation" instead of looking more broadly at all the numerous apocalyptic "predictions" of the Roman/Jewish conflagration which we have discussed in the chapter on Luke: predictions of the world ablaze, of family conflict, of the toppling of the stones of the temple, of the sudden disappearances of women as they work side by side, of the gathering of vultures over carcasses, of war and insurrection, etc. It is true that the "abomination" has a more limited meaning, but to interpret it with precision should not require dismissing any allusion to the Jewish War as a "vague apocalyptic."[4] We shall return to this idea of referential specificity in a moment.

The second area of perplexity arises when we consider the nature of apocalyptic eschatology as we have it in the Book of Daniel and the synoptic gospels. Matthew 24:15, the source of the "vague apocalyptic," makes explicit reference to the Book of Daniel. The "abomination of desolation" is that "of which the prophet Daniel spoke," says the gospel, and it is something that will "stand in the holy place." The sense is of desecration or profanation of the temple, and when we turn back to Daniel, we find this precise meaning in at least two of the three references to the abomination. In Daniel 11:31, it is predicted that a future king who is attacking the Holy Covenant will send armed forces to "desecrate the sanctuary and the citadel and do away with the regular offering. And there they will set up 'the abominable thing that causes desolation.'" Then, in Chapter 12:11, the text refers to an eschatological or "end time" during which "the regular offering is abolished and 'the abomination of desolation' is set up". These two references apparently depict the same desecration, but in neither case does the author of Daniel refer specifically to Jerusalem nor to any particular time period, except as may be inferred by starting with the year or time period in which Daniel receives his visions, and then counting the number of rulers he mentions and estimating the approximate time period from the result. It would take a greater scholar than I am to achieve a numerical result using this technique. However, I am able to note that the visions are given to us as having been received "[i]n the third year of Cyrus king of Persia" — which occurred during the Babylonian captivity in the Sixth Century B.C.E. (A previous vision during the reign of Darius does make specific reference to Jerusalem as to the calamity which has already befallen, i.e., the Babylonian exile, see Dan. 9:12.) The author of Daniel then refers to four kings and to events said to be far in the future. We add to these facts the fact that our author is believed to have written in 165 B.C.E., and the fact that, in the manner of apocalyptic literature, he is using the distant past as a springboard for his prophet's "predictions" about a future time which actually has occurred prior to the book's composition. In short, the apocalypse writer uses fictional history to make topical observations about his own time, without necessarily risking his political neck thereby.

At this point, we should note that this technique is exactly the same one used by the gospel authors, most especially Luke.

Please note that the "predictions" in the gospels are no more or less specific than those in Daniel. However, since it is evidently known that Antiochus Epiphanes in 168 B.C.E. erected a statue of Zeus in the Holy of Holies, Wilson *accepts* the prophecy of the Book of Daniel regarding the "abomination of desolation" as a topical reference to this desecration of the temple, which occurred two or three years before the composition of Daniel. But he *rejects* the same result (a topical allusion) when applied to the apocalyptic "prediction" in the synoptic gospels. Why? There are no specific references, he says. But nothing in the Book of Daniel makes specific reference to the events of 168 B.C.E. Why is one non-specific apocalyptic allusion acceptable while another one is not?

Obviously, time was not even reckoned in numbered years in the ancient world. The concept of "Anno Domini" was invented by Dionysus Exiguus some five hundred thirty-one years after Dionysus' own calculation of the Year 1.[6] As we see again and again in the various books of the Bible, historical time is identified by such event-markers as "In the third year of the reign of Jehoiakim king of Judah," (Dan.1:1); "In the first year of Belshazzar king of Babylon," (Dan. 7:1); "In the twelfth year of the reign of Nebuchadnezzar," (Jud. 1:1); "… during the reign of Herod," (Matt.2:1) "… in the days of Ahasuerus, the Ahasuerus who ruled from India to Ethiopia, a hundred and twenty-seven provinces," (Esther 1:1); "In the beginning of creation," (Gen.1:1). Moreover, in an apocalyptic work, references to the topical event are deliberately blurred, because prophets spoke in a deliberately open-ended, cryptic way. This is why the criticism that "running to the hills" is a bad tactic in a prophetic statement is absurd. The language of prophecy is symbolic (consider all the monstrous allegorical creatures in Daniel or in the Book of Revelation), suggestive (the vultures and the carcasses), based on an under-standing of the future time in the mind of the prophet which does not translate into precise facts, dates, and strategies available to the tactical interests of the prophet's audience. But in apocalyptic literature, the cryptic description of the future time constitutes a tacit understanding between the prophet and the readers of the literature, who validate the symbols by means of filling in the blanks with their own contemporary knowledge. In short, the very ambiguity in the words of the prophet give the prophecy its mimetic verisimilitude; it is ambiguity at which the author of the apocalyptic aims. And yet that ambiguity is never obscure. The work relies on the temporal knowledge of the reader, and the "inner" meaning of the prophecy is deciphered with certainty.

If Wilson's criticism were limited to pointing out that the "abomination of desolation" rather clearly suggests the erection of a pagan idol in the temple, and that therefore it is not an allusion to the entire Jewish War of 66-70 C.E., I would agree with him. But in the context of a gospel apocalypse which alludes repeatedly to scenes which cannot possibly fail to evoke that tribal disaster in the minds of the gospel readers of the late first and early second century, it seems to me that he misses the synechdochic function which the "abomination" has: it is a part that stands for the whole, when taken together with other parts of the whole. It would be like addressing an audience of European Jews in 1946 or 1956 and referring to the "abomination of the breaking glass." The image might have specific reference to Krystallnacht, but that image would conjure up everything else that had followed Krystallnacht, of which that horrible night was only a precursor.

I am aware that I might be committing an anachronistic error by assuming that the readers of the gospels in the first and second centuries would all have knowledge of the Jerusalem disaster of 70 C.E. and would experience it with a common sense of tragedy. This was not a world, after all, with round-the-clock news coverage. But given the recurrence in Christian literature of this period of the tensions arising from diaspora and from doctrinal adjustments and negotiations between ethnic Jews and non-ethnic "People of God," or between the Jerusalem church of Peter and the mission to the gentiles of Paul and so on, I find it much less difficult to accept that all Jews and Christians in the post-war Greco-Roman world had a keen perception of the tragedy than that they really hadn't noticed it much, or would not think of it in connection with all the images of death, destruction, horror, massed armies at the gates, etc. which pepper the gospels like a fine seasoning.

The contextual reading that I am arguing for here is one that groups together the exhortation to "head for the hills" (Matt.24:16) with the warning that no one on the roof should bother to go downstairs when they see all the apocalyptic signs (Matt.24:17). At the same time as false idols are set up in the temple, the temple is destroyed, wars and rumors of wars occur, false prophets arise — and "the end will come" (Matt.24:2, 6, 11, 14). The prediction is not offered as a defensive military tactic, but as a poetic rendering of the moment when time stops and earthly life no longer means anything. The sun darkens and the Son of Adam comes on the clouds (Matt. 24:29-30). But "no one knows" the exact day, not even the Son. Only the Father knows (Matt.24:36). The Father only, at the time Jesus makes the prediction — and all the readers of the book, who have since experienced or at least heard of the end of the world, and (if we want to complete the symbolism) who have experienced also a kind of parousia in the form of a new religious dispensation. Of course, the parousia would come to be interpreted as remaining in the future. That is the kind of ahistorical reading that comes into play when the reader loses touch with topical references or symbols engendered by topical issues.

Chapter 8

Conclusion

The manuscript for this book began, many years ago, as a series of attempts to read the various canonical gospels as if they were little novels, works of literature with coherent and intentional structures, the meaning derivable from that narratological coherence: beginning, middle, end, chronological development. I was never so naive as to suppose that such an approach had ever been intended for these books by the church. I grew up a Christian. Anyone who has ever spent time in a Christian church knows that the gospels are never read as a series of ordered events forming a narrative whole. Instead they are read with a kind of dogged incoherence, focusing for an entire service on tiny snippets taken out of context. Moreover, certain selections have seasonal significance. The birth stories of Matthew and Luke are emphasized at Christmas; the stone rolls away from the tomb at Easter, and so on. In fact, we have already discussed the more orthodox sense of structure which argues that the gospels are not so much books but a series of occasional readings, lections, chapters and verses which are dipped into for liturgical moments. Obviously, if we understand the gospels that way, it makes no difference whether Peter and John observe Jesus raising a dead girl in one chapter and in the next seem dumbfounded by the very concept of resurrection. That juxtaposition is dramatically incoherent only if we assume that meaning derives from the order of events in a story that is read as a whole; that is, if we read these stories as if they were literary fictions.

The fact that they were never intended to be literary fictions means little to me. Despite their intended purpose, they are, in fact, in a sense, literary fictions. They are myths which are written down, and told as if they were events that happened.

This makes them like literary fictions — like little novels.

Treating them as if they were little novels—while at the same time being aware of their prior treatment by theologians as if they were little histories – raises questions about how we think of fiction, how we think of history, and how we think of religion. The experiment has demonstrated, I hope, that critical reading of a work of fiction opens windows to truth claims at a very basic level: the level of the definition of the text (what is it?); the level of when and how it was composed (what was going on at the time, and how is the text affected by topical events?); the level of form (what genre is it?). These are questions for the literary critic, and they lead to factual assumptions. The idea that studying fiction with the mind of a literary critic is an exercise removed from fact claims is completely without merit.

It is not literariness that is opposed to historicity, but rather a concept of metaphysical or absolutist truth. The historicist view is one that says that the artifact (whatever it is) comes out of a particular place and time, a particular orientation, and is not simply an objective revelation, or a messsage from the mind of God. The nature of the work, and the facts surrounding its composition, will tell us about the facts or fantasies out of which that nature was woven. Concepts of absolute truth, not being open to questioning by the rational mind, close the mind off from such inquiry.

Literary awareness is the best revealer of historical facts when dealing with the gospels, because the text is ninety-nine percent of what we have to work with. But our interest transcends searches for facts; we seek also an understanding of the deepest meaning, which does not come from deliberate, orthodox submission to incoherence. It comes, rather, from curiosity and intellectual pursuit.

Religious people would disagree on that last point, but this is not a religious book; and even on that point, I believe I am not totally opposed to religious writers such as Bishop Spong. The gospels are dead unless we learn to do something new with them. But they need not die, because in fact they are incredibly rich if we care to approach them with an open mind. I disagree with those who suggest that reading the gospels is only done by an act of submission to revelation. That is no more than to shut off one's mind, something which strikes me as against the grain of the apostle Paul's exhortation in 1 Corinthians 14:20 to avoid childish thinking. Why is it that so much academic discussion of the "Bible as literature" never actually says very much? Is it because there is a fear of reading outside the accustomed acts of submission? Isn't it this same fear that makes people go to study groups when they want to learn about the Bible, instead of simply sitting down and reading it with a concentrated mind? As long as this fear dominates us, we will never really read our Bibles. We will simply keep them as talismans on our mantels.

The conclusions of this book should by now be clear to the reader. First, there is no history to be found in the work of theologians writing in the school of "historical criticism," which means all the books with reference to the "historical Jesus." Second, the oft-stated assertion by these critics that literary criticism has no means of testing truth claims is a false assertion, made from ignorance of literary criticism. Third, a comparison of the content of recurring themes in the canonical gospels reveals that incidents in the myth are tropes that are re-worked from one version to another, one prominent example being the episode in Bethany which became, in John, the story of the resurrection of Lazarus.

The former conclusions proceed from an examination of the content of the gospels. The remaining chief conclusions of my book result from a consideration of genre. Taking the scholarly consensus for the dates of composition of the gospels, we arrive at the conclusion that they are essentially Jewish apocalyptic texts, based on the way such texts work, with three points in time as referents. Seen as apocalyptic "predictors" of the Jewish War

of 70 C.E., the gospels thus define for us their own cultural significance as the urge toward survival of a dying (Jewish) culture,
seeking to escape its fate by amalgamation into the gentile
population of the Hellenized Roman Empire – a successful
strategy, as it turned out.

History is something that must be imagined. Orthodoxy
blocks the imagination. I am asking those readers who care to do
so – and only those readers — to try unblocking their imaginations. I have asked readers to try to imagine that the real world of
the First Century C.E. was like the present world in terms of the
physical laws that apply to it. Indeed, if it really were somehow
different, the ancient world would have no concept of a miracle.
Starting with that view, then, imagine what it means that it took
thirty-seven years from the time Jesus was supposedly resurrected from the dead for someone to write down the story of his
life. Paul was preaching the resurrection before that, but the
virgin birth, the loaves and fishes, the resurrection of Lazarus, the
healing of the blind and the lame, and all the other wonders and
preachments were not committed to writing for a period of time
comparable to that between the bombing of Pearl Harbor in 1941
and the year 1978. (Longer, in the case of the Lazarus story in its
most famous form.)

Continue this process. Consider that Christianity began as a
Jewish sect, and did not split from Judaism, so we are told, until
about 88 C.E. Jews wrote the first two gospels, at least: to judge
from the content, most certainly Mark and Matthew. Mark was
probably composed about 70 C.E., which was the last year of the
Jewish War, when the temple at Jerusalem was destroyed by the
Romans, and Jews were crucified *en masse*. Is it delusional to
imagine that Jews in Roman-dominated Palestine would have
been aware of this devastation, through word of mouth, and
would have considered it of some significance at that time? So
much so, in fact, that a story alluding to the destruction of the
temple — and to death, vultures, carcasses, and *crucifixion* —

would have created an inescapable echo in the minds of Jews of that era?

Notes

Introduction

1. *See, e.g.,* Spong, *RBF* 213-14.

2. Spong, *RBF* 31-33.

3. The "hesitation" is one between accepting a fantastic premise or a more realistic explanation of seemingly fantastic events. This theory occurs in *The Fantastic, passim.* My own treatment of the gospels is not consistent with Todorov's theory of the fantastic, because, for Todorov, allegory and fantasy are discrete, non-overlapping categories. However, my treatment of the Acts would be consistent with Todorov's theory.

4. Keith Hopkins, *A World Full of Gods: The Strange Triumph of Christianity,* NY: Free p 2000:4.

5. This condensed summary comes out of nearly all the sources I read for this book. Perhaps the best single source for these ideas is the remarkably compact work by Antonia Tripolitis. See Works Cited.

6. *Of Grammatology* 71.

7. Nor is the idea stable from one reference to another. Tripolitis, for example, notes that *for the Stoics* the universe was ruled by a supreme cosmic power, "a fiery substance that the Stoics called Logos, Divine Reason, or God. The Logos is the organizing, integrating, and energizing principle of the whole universe." *RHRA* 37. Despite the similarities of this idea to those discussed in my book, this definition is obviously not the same as the others in every respect. Notably distinct here is the fiery substance, which obviously makes one think of the Roman "sol invictus," or of Mithraism, both of which were forms of sun worship. There is simply no bottom to this concept of Logos.

8. Hans-Georg Gadamer, *Truth and Method,* 2d rev. ed., Tr. Joel

Weinsheimer and Donald G. Marshall, NY: Continuum (pap.) 1998: 456-57.

Chapter 1. Literary Criticism and the Historical Jesus

1. Edgar Krentz, *The Historical-Critical Method*, Philadelphia: Fortress P 1975: 17, 61.
2. Krentz 2, 49.
3. Krentz 49-50.
4. John P. Meier, *A Marginal Jew: Rethinking the Historical Jesus*, v.1, NY/London, etc.: Doubleday 1991: 12. This "willingness to die" remark, while quite true, seems really in the nature of an unexamined assumption of historicity aimed at our sense of ethics or our emotions. One need only look at yesterday's and today's news to see the wide range of questionable beliefs for which significant numbers of people have been willing to die – religious inspiration seems peculiarly prone to producing such willingness – to suspect that the willingness to die for a religious belief may not be the best yardstick for judging the *historical* validity of fact claims underlying that belief. Wishing as much as possible not to offend, I trust that the reader can easily supply his or her own examples.
5. Meier 12.
6. Albert Schweitzer, *The Quest of the Historical Jesus*, New York: Macmillan 1964.
7. Schweitzer 403; Krentz 17.
8. Meier 198.
9. Meier 21-24.
10. Frederick Copleston, S.J. *A History of Philosophy*, v.1, Part 1. Westminster, MD: Newman P 1962 (orig. 1946): Ch. 3.1.
11. The principle is applied throughout the *Anatomy*. In fact, however, I believe Frye actually stated it as an explicit principle in an oft-collected essay entitled "The Keys to Dreamland."

12. I can hear readers objecting, "But is it fair to imply that these sources are 'literary works?'" My answer is yes, because the principle here cited applies to "works of literature" in the largest sense – *i.e.,* to written documents – as much as it does to "literary works" in the narrow sense which one might associate with a work such as Frye's, namely, deliberately fictive, poetic, or belletrist works of more modern times. I recognize – indeed, the patient reader will come to understand that it is part of my larger point – that we are dealing with works (Diogenes and the NT) fundamentally different from one another and different from later literature.

13. Jakobson's application associated third person with epic, first person with lyric, etc. My reliance is on Todorov.

14. There are so many editions of Grimms that I think a citation would not help the reader, who need only examine the opening lines of these and many other Grimms tales in any edition. Language of this sort is less common in Hans Christian Andersen, although it does appear. Andersen's genre appears to be in between the traditional fairy tale and the short story, although I must defer to others on points so highly specific to the fairy tale.

15. An interesting critique of this whole concept has been advanced by Richard Rorty, who is influenced by Wittgenstein. Rorty's ideas would seem to tend toward a greater emphasis on historicity as opposed to concepts of metaphysical truth, and insofar as that may be an accurate perception, I see my own essay as consistent with that emphasis. But this gets us off on a new subject. The point here is simply that mimesis has a history of being a subject of literary critical analysis, most famously in Aristotle and Auerbach.

16. All or nearly all of the examples appear at various places in Spong's book. It is possible that I may have added the jar of flour.

17. Goulder also makes reference to Deut. 4:37.

18. I am using Luke for purposes of explication here. Other gospels also suggest the same heterotelic function. *See, e.g.,* Mark 13, Matthew 24, John 11:47-48.

19. Meier disagrees with the thesis that "parthenos" is necessarily a mistranslation of "almah," (Meier 221-22). Spong accepts the thesis of a mistranslation (Spong 188-89). Another who accepts it is Prof. Gize Vermes (226-28). Vermes' discussion is the most enlightening of the three, in my view.

20. The reference is to J. Enoch Powell, *The Evolution of the Gospel.* See Chapter 7.

Chapter 2. Matthew

1. *See, e.g.,* Geza Vermes, *The Changing Faces of Jesus,* NY: Penguin 2001: 226-230.

2. For a discussion of the details of these virgin births, see Timothy Freke and Peter Gandy, *The Jesus Mysteries,* NY: Three Rivers P 1999: 29-30.

3. Fictional thinking often requires that such questions are best resolved with a view toward dramatic irony. Thus, in Robert Graves' novel, *King Jesus,* the father of Jesus turns out to be Herod Antipas! Needless to say, this is a re-telling, and not an interpretation of the gospels. See Graves, *King Jesus,* NY: Farrar, Straus & Giroux, 1946.

4. Discussed at length in Chapter 6 of Vermes.

5. Herod died shortly before Passover in 4 B.C.E., according to Josephus, *The Jewish War,* tr. G.A. Williamson, NY: Penguin, rev. 1981: 118, 424, n.35. Hereinafter *JW.* I have used the Penguin edition not only for this note, but because of a fondness for the translation. The more traditional Loeb edition will be cited hereinafter as *JW (Loeb),* with book and line numbers.

6. *JW* 133; *JW (Loeb)* II:119 *et seq.*

7. *JW* 42; *JW (Loeb)* I:110-112.
8. *JW* 137-38; *JW (Loeb)* II:162-165.
9. *JW* 137-38; *JW (Loeb)* II:164-65.
10. *ASV* n.26:61, p.109. Robert J. Miller, ed., *The Complete Gospels: Annotated Scholars Version*, Sonoma, CA: Polebridge P 1992. The HarperCollins pap. ed., 1994, is used here. Hereinafter *ASV*.
11. It would appear that there is consensus about this interpretation. However, the Book of Daniel itself is set entirely in the period of the Babylonian exile in the Sixth Century B.C.E. This interpretation must therefore be an extrapolation of the visionary dreams of Daniel, which extend far into the future from the time of Belshazzar, the son of Nebuchednazzar. The book was actually written circa 165 B.C.E.
12. Tripolitis tells us: "Jewish apocalyptic literature flourished and enjoyed an enormous popularity both within Palestine and the Diaspora between 200 B.C.E. and 90 C.E. ... The apocalypticists continued the tradition of the prophets by adopting the major themes of the prophetic teachings, in particular the prediction element, and incorporated them into a novel world-historical, cosmic form. Many apocalyptic works were written during times of hardship and oppression. These conditions were depicted by the writers in a cosmic setting, perceived not only as a local or national situation but one of universal significance, and accompanied by supernatural signs. ... " *RHRA* 69-70.
13. *ASV* n.24:15, p.102.
14. See, *e.g.*, Miles 233.
15. "Actual" does not mean historical; it means fictionally plausible.

Chapter 3. Luke

1. The gospel translations in this article are all from Robert J. Miller, ed., *The Complete Gospels, Annotated Scholar's Version*,

rev. ed., HarperSanFrancisco 1994. All references are to Luke except where noted. Other Biblical references are to the NEB.

2. For a discussion of the qualities of the ascetic communist sect called the Essenes, see Josephus, *JW (Loeb)* beginning at II:119.

3. *See, e.g.,* Geza Vermes, *The Changing Faces of Jesus,* NY: Penguin 2001: 127, 161.

4. *JW* Book V. The Loeb introduction to Books I and II dates the publication in Greek of *JW* to between 75-79 C.E. (xii).

5. *JW* IV:107, 391, 289, respectively.

6. *JW* VI:276-77.

7. *JW* VI:308-315.

Chapter 4. John

1. *Against Heresies* (aka *On the Detection and Refutation of the Knowledge Falsely So Called)* 28.4 & 28.5, in Robert M. Grant, *Irenaeus of Lyons,* London/New York: Routledge 1997. Hereinafter *AH.*

2. Tripolitis 37.

3. Tripolitis 79.

4. Jacques Derrida, *Of Grammatology,* tr. Gayatri Chakravorty Spivak (corr. ed.), Baltimore/London: Johns Hopkins UP 1997:11, 13-14.

5. However, Irenaeus makes the point that Gnosticism had no tradition, but was simply the growth of self-invented concepts introduced by the Gnostic exegetes and snake oil salesmen, as he clearly thought of them. These arguments are to be found in the refutations of Book II of *AH.*

6. *AH* I:15.3; 30.12-13.

7. The ASV notes point out that *"Woman* is abrupt and disrespectful, and the question is the same as that used by demons to address Jesus in Mark 1:24 and Luke 4:34 … " *See* the note to 2.4, p.203.

8. Miles 153-54.

9. The Special Laws III, X:(58). *The Works of Philo*, tr. C.D. Yonge, Peabody, MA: Hendrickson 1993:600.

10. Richard A. Horsley with John S. Hanson, *Bandits, Prophets & Messiahs: Popular Movements in the Time of Jesus,* Harrisburg, PA: Trinity P International 1999:35.

11. Horsley 88.

12. Horsley 245.

13. Burton L. Mack, *Who Wrote the New Testament?* San Francisco: Harper SF 1995:182.

Chapter 5. Mark

1. Scholars apparently disagree about the order of composition of Luke and John, with some placing Luke last, some John. Most seem to agree that Mark was the first and Matthew the second, although some place Matthew and Luke at about the same time. Eusebius (87) places John's gospel as definitely the last, written in reaction to all three of the others and as a deliberate improvement on them. My argument about the order of composition does not rest entirely on the scholarship, but on the nature of the development of the "stopover in Bethany" episode.

2. It is precisely this ability to distinguish the real from the unreal that separates fantastic literature from myth in the theory of Tzvetan Todorov. See his *The Fantastic*, Tr. Richard Howard, Ithaca; Cornell UP 1975: 116 *et seq.* Reader identification with a character who hesitates to believe what seems unreal is also the first defining characteristic of such literature, according to Todorov; and this is exactly what is being described here.

3. In Todorov's scheme, the choice would be to accept either a rational explanation or the supernatural one. If we accepted a rational explanation, the story would be classified as "uncanny," whereas if we (or the identified character) accepted the supernatural explanation, the story would be

classfied as "marvelous." See Note 2.

Chapter 6. The Fantastic History of the Apostles

1. I am speaking, of course, about a double sense that is entirely conscious on the part of the believer. The lack of a single sense of orientation to reality which is *not* willed, is, by definition, characteristic of psychosis, as Todorov has observed. See *The Fantastic* at 115.

2. E.M. Forster, *Aspects of the Novel*, NY/London: Harcourt Brace Jovanovich 1955 (pap), (orig. 1927): 27.

3. Todorov, *The Fantastic* 60.

4. Robert Harris, *Fatherland*, NY: Random House 1992.

5. Bede, *A History of the English Church and People*, Tr. Leo Sherley-Price, rev. R.E. Latham, NY: Penguin 1986:46-47 (1.7).

6. Todorov, *The Fantastic* 116.

7. Sigmund Freud, *Civilization and Its Discontents*, Tr. James Strachey, NY: W.W. Norton, 1962:12.

8. The NEB reads: "and in the act of blessing he parted from them." (Lk 24:51.) A note says: *"Some witnesses add* and was carried up into heaven." The ASV, which has been the text of choice for this book, contains the ascension.

9. John Shelby Spong, *Rescuing the Bible from Fundamentalism*, SF: HarperSanFrancisco 1992 (pap): 94.

10. "The feelings excited by improper art are kinetic, desire or loathing." *See* Chapter V. James Joyce, *A Portrait of the Artist as a Young Man*. Ed. Chester G. Anderson, NY: Viking P, 1968 (pap): 205.

11. Northrop Frye, *Anatomy of Criticism*, Princeton UP 1973 (orig. 1957) (pap): 186-88.

12. "There are approximately fifteen major speeches in Acts, most of them rather lengthy." Burton L. Mack, *Who Wrote the New Testament?* SF: Harper San Francisco (pap.) 1996:232.

13. Eusebius, *The History of the Church from Christ to Constantine*,

Tr. G.A. Williamson, rev. ed. Andrew Louth, NY/London: Penguin (pap.) 1989:67 (III.4).

Chapter 7. A Vague Apocalyptic?

1. A.N. Wilson, *Paul: The Mind of the Apostle,* NY/London: W.W. Norton 1997:252-53. Wilson's reference is to J. Enoch Powell, *The Evolution of the Gospel,* New Haven, CT: Yale UP 1994.
2. Wilson 253-56.
3. Wilson 253.
4. Wilson 253.
5. Wilson 90.
6. David Ewing Duncan, *Calendar,* NY: Avon 1998: 91-92.

Works Cited

Andersen, Hans. *Fairy Tales & Legends.* London: Bodley Head 1967.

Angus, S. *The Mystery-Religions: A Study in the Religious Background of Early Christianity.* NY: Dover 1975.

Aristotle, *Poetics.* Tr. S. H. Butcher, Intr. Francis Fergusson. NY: Hill & Wang 1961.

Auerbach, Eric. *Mimesis.* Tr. Willard Trask. Princeton UP 1953.

Bede. *A History of the English Church and People.* Tr. Leo Sherley-Price. Rev. R.E. Latham. NY: Penguin (pap) 1986. Bible editions: ASV: Robert J. Miller, ed. *The Complete Gospels: Annotated Scholars Version.* Rev. ed. SF: HarperSanFrancisco 1994 (pap. ed. [orig. Polebridge Press 1992, see Acknowledgements]). NEB: *The New English Bible with the Apocrypha.* NY: Cambridge UP 1972. NKJV: (New King James Version). Nashville: Thomas Nelson 1990.

Bulgakov, Mikhail. *The Master and Margarita.* Tr. Diana Burgin and Katherine Tiernan O'Connor, with Annotations/Afterword by Ellenda Proffer. NY: Random House/Vintage 1996.

Collins, John J. *The Apocalyptic Imagination: An Introduction to Jewish Apocalyptic Literature.* 2d Ed. Grand Rapids, MI/Cambridge, UK: William B. Eerdmans; Livonia, MI: Dove Booksellers 1998.

Copleston, Frederick, S.J. *A History of Philosophy,* v.1, Part 1. Westminster, MD: Newman P 1962 (orig. 1946).

Derrida, Jacques. *Of Grammatology.* Tr. Gayatri Chakravorty Spivak. Corr. Ed. (pap.) Baltimore/London: Johns Hopkins UP 1997.

Diogenes Laertius. *Lives of Eminent Philosophers,* v.1. Tr. R.D. Hicks. Cambridge/London: Harvard UP (Loeb) 2000.

Duncan, David Ewing. *Calendar.* NY: Avon (pap) 1998.

Eusebius. *The History of the Church from Christ to Constantine.* Tr. G.A. Williamson. Rev./ed./Intro. by Andrew Louth. NY/London (pap) 1989.

Forster, E.M. *Aspects of the Novel.* NY/London: Harcourt Brace Jovanovich (pap) 1955.

Freke, Timothy and Gandy, Peter. *The Jesus Mysteries: Was the "Original Jesus" a Pagan God?* NY: Three Rivers P 1999.

Freud, Sigmund. *Civilization and Its Discontents.* Tr./Ed. James Strachey. (pap) NY: W.W. Norton 1962.

Frye, Northrop. *Anatomy of Criticism.* Princeton UP 1973 (pap.) (orig. 1957).

Gadamer, Hans-Georg. *Truth and Method.* 2d Rev. Ed. Tr. Rev. Joel Weisheimer and Donald G. Marshall. NY: Continuum (pap) 1998.

Gibbon, Edward. *The History of the Decline and Fall of the Roman Empire.* 3 vols. Ed. David Womersley. London/NY: Allen Lane/Penguin P 1994.

Gifford, Edward Winslow, *et al,* eds. *Californian Indian Nights.* Lincoln & London: U of NE P 1985.

Goulder, M.D. *Midrash & Lection in Matthew.* London: SPCK 1974.

Grant, Robert M. *Irenaeus of Lyons.* London/NY: Routledge 1997.

Graves, Robert. *King Jesus.* NY: Farrar, Straus, Giroux/Noonday P (pap) 1992.

Grimm, Jacob & Wilhelm. *The Complete Illustrated Stories of The Brothers Grimm.* London: Chancellor P 1990.

Harris, Robert. *Fatherland.* NY: Random House 1992.

Hayes, John H. *Introduction to the Bible.* Philadelphia: Westminster P 1971.

Hesiod. *The Theogony.* Tr. Norman O. Brown. NY: Liberal Arts P (pap) 1953.

Hopkins, Keith. *A World Full of Gods: The Strange Triumph of Christianity.* NY: Free P 2000.

Horsley, Richard A. with John S. Hanson. *Bandits, Prophets and*

Messiahs: Popular Movements in the Time of Jesus. Harrisburg, PA: Trinity P Internatl (pap) 1999.

Hume, David. "Of Miracles" in *Essays Moral, Political & Literary*. Oxford UP 1963 (pap): 519-44.

Irenaeus. *Against Heresies. See* Grant, Robert M.

Jameson, Frederic. *Postmodernism, or, The Cultural Logic of Late Capitalism*. Durham, NC: Duke UP 1994.

Josephus. *The Jewish War*. Tr. H. St. J. Thackeray. Cambridge/London: Harvard UP (Loeb) 1997. *The Jewish War*. Tr. G.A. Williamson. Rev. by E. Mary Smallwood. NY/London: Penguin (pap) 1970.

Joyce, James. *A Portrait of the Artist as a Young Man*. Chester G. Anderson, ed. Viking P (pap) 1974.

Krentz, Edgar. *The Historical-Critical Method*. Philadelphia, PA: Fortress P 1975.

Mack, Burton. *Who Wrote the New Testament?* SF: HarperSanFrancisco (pap) 1995.

Mallarmé, Stephane. *Selected Poems*. Tr. C.F. MacIntyre. Berkeley & LA: U CA P 1957.

Meier, John P. *A Marginal Jew: Rethinking the Historical Jesus*, v.1. NY/London, etc.: Doubleday 1991.

Miles, Jack. *Christ: A Crisis in the Life of God*. NY: Knopf 2001.

Miller, Robert J. See Bible editions.

Neihardt, John G. *Black Elk Speaks*. Lincoln: U NE P (pap)1961.

Philo of Alexandria. *The Works of Philo*. Tr. C.D. Yonge. Peabody, MA: Hendrickson 1993.

Powell, J. Enoch. *The Evolution of the Gospel*. New Haven, CT: Yale UP 1994.

Rorty, Richard. *Philosophy and the Mirror of Nature*. Princeton UP (pap) 1980.

Schweitzer, Albert. *The Quest of the Historical Jesus*. NY: Macmillan 1964.

Spong, John Shelby. *Liberating the Gospels*. SF: HarperSanFrancisco 1996. *Rescuing the Bible from*

Fundamentalism. SF: HarperSanFrancisco (pap) 1992.

Tacitus. *The Annals of Imperial Rome.* Tr. Michael Grant. Rev. ed. NY: Barnes & Noble 1971.

Tedlock, Dennis, Tr. *Popol Vuh.* NY, etc.: Simon & Schuster (pap) 1985.

Todorov, Tzvetan. *The Fantastic: A Structural Approach to a Literary Genre.* Tr. Richard Howard. Fwd. by Robert Scholes. Ithaca, NY: Cornell UP (pap) 1975. *Theories of the Symbol.* Tr. Catherine Porter. Ithaca: Cornell UP 1984.

Tripolitis, Antonía. *Religions of the Hellenistic-Roman Age.* Grand Rapids/Cambridge (pap), UK: Eerdmans 2002.

Vermes, Giza. *The Changing Faces of Jesus.* NY:Penguin Compass (pap) 2001.

Wilson, A.N. *Paul: The Mind of the Apostle.* NY/London: W.W. Norton 1997.

CHRISTIAN
ALTERNATIVE

Throughout the two thousand years of Christian tradition there
have been, and still are, groups and individuals that exist in the
margins and upon the edge of faith. But in Christianity's
contrapuntal history it has often been these outcasts and
pioneers that have forged contemporary orthodoxy out of
former radicalism as belief evolves to engage with and
encompass the ever-changing social and scientific realities. Real
faith lies not in the comfortable certainties of the Orthodox, but
somewhere in a half-glimpsed hinterland on the dirt track to
Emmaus, where the Death of God meets the Resurrection, where
the supernatural Christ meets the historical Jesus, and where the
revolution liberates both the oppressed and the oppressors.

Welcome to Christian Alternative... a space at the edge where
the light shines through.